Amirul Sheikh

SOFTWARE ARCHITECTURE: CREATE SOFTWARE LIKE A PRO

A Comprehensive Guide to Become a Master in Software Development

Dedication

To the architects of innovation —
This book is for the dreamers who transform ideas into systems,
the builders who embrace complexity with clarity,
and the teams who collaborate to create what seems impossible.

To every mentor who has guided with wisdom,
every peer who has challenged with questions,
and every learner who dares to ask "what if?" —
this is dedicated to you.

May your designs inspire, your systems endure,
and your passion for creating never waver.

PROLOGUE

Software architecture is the foundation of every successful system, shaping its scalability, performance, and resilience. In today's fast-evolving world, designing adaptable and maintainable architectures is not just a technical necessity —it's the key to driving innovation.

This book takes you on a journey into the core principles, patterns, and practices of software architecture. Whether you're a beginner seeking to understand the basics or an experienced professional exploring advanced topics like microservices, event-driven systems, or domain-driven design, this book offers valuable insights for all levels.

Through a blend of theory, real-world examples, and practical exercises, you'll learn to craft architectures that solve complex challenges while aligning with business goals. From foundational patterns to integrating modern practices like DevOps and cloud-native design, this book provides the tools to create scalable, efficient, and resilient systems.

More than just technical guidance, this book celebrates the art of collaboration—bridging the gap between developers, stakeholders, and business leaders. Wherever you are in your journey, this is your guide to building systems that not only succeed today but endure the challenges of tomorrow.

Table of Content

FOUNDATIONS OF SOFTWARE ARCHITECTURE

Introduces the fundamental principles and mindset required to become a high-performance programmer. Whether you are a seasoned software engineer or just beginning your journey, mastering these principles will set the stage for a successful career in building efficient, scalable, and maintainable software systems. The focus is on understanding what makes programming "high-performance" and why it matters in today's software-driven world.

This module serves as a gateway to the world of software architecture, introducing learners to its core concepts, significance, and the role it plays in modern software development. Whether you are a beginner or have a few years of programming experience, this module will help you understand what makes software architecture a critical discipline and how it contributes to building robust, scalable, and maintainable systems.

The module begins with an overview of what software architecture is, comparing it to related concepts like software design and implementation. You will learn why software architecture is essential for aligning technical solutions with business goals and ensuring the long-term success of a system.

We will then explore the responsibilities of a software architect, including the technical and non-technical skills required for this role. This will provide learners with an understanding of how architects bridge the gap between technical teams and stakeholders, as well as provides learners with the skills necessary for making critical decisions that influence the entire project lifecycle.

The module also highlights the value of architecture in creating scalable systems that meet functional and non-functional requirements, such as performance, reliability, and security. By the end of the module, learners will appreciate how software architecture affects every layer of a project, from planning to deployment and beyond.

The lessons provide clear, actionable insights and examples, ensuring that both beginners and experienced professionals can follow along. Through engaging discussions and practical exercises, this module lays the foundation for deeper exploration into software architecture.

Lesson 1.1: What is Software Architecture?

Software architecture is the backbone of any software system. It defines the high-level structure, guiding principles, and design decisions that determine how a software system will function and evolve over time. Think of it as the blueprint for building a complex system—it provides a clear plan to ensure the system is robust, scalable, and meets both business and technical requirements.

Defining Software Architecture

At its core, software architecture is about the **organization of a system**. It describes how components interact, how data flows through the system, and how non-functional requirements like performance, security, and scalability are addressed. While software design focuses on individual components and their details, architecture deals with the big picture.

For instance, consider a city. The urban planning represents the architecture: where roads, schools, and neighborhoods are located. On the other hand, the design of an individual house corresponds to software design. The architecture ensures that all the houses connect harmoniously to the city's water, electricity, and road systems, enabling efficient operation.

Why Software Architecture is Important

Software architecture provides multiple benefits:

1. **Guidance for Development Teams:** It serves as a roadmap for developers, defining what needs to be built and how components interact.

2. **Improved Scalability and Maintainability:** A well-thought-out architecture makes it easier to scale systems as users' needs grow and to adapt to changes with minimal effort.

3. **Risk Management:** By identifying potential bottlenecks or vulnerabilities early, it mitigates risks before they become costly issues.

4. **Alignment with Business Goals:** Architecture ensures that the technical design aligns with the organization's strategic objectives, enabling faster delivery and better Return on Investment (ROI).

Software Architecture vs. Design

Software architecture is not the same as software design, although they overlap:

- **Architecture** defines the overall structure: high-level decisions like choosing between *monolithic, distributed,* or *micro-services* architectures.

- **Design** focuses on details within components: selecting *data structures* or *algorithms* for specific modules.

For example, in a web application, the architecture may decide to use a micro-services-based structure, while the design determines how the user authentication module stores passwords securely.

Examples of Good and Bad Software Architecture

A good software architecture supports long-term goals while addressing immediate needs. For instance, Netflix's transition to a micro-services architecture allowed it to scale its streaming service globally and improve uptime significantly.

On the other hand, bad architecture leads to issues such as **"spaghetti code,"** where the system becomes hard to understand, modify, or extend. Many legacy systems suffer from this, resulting in skyrocketing maintenance costs and frequent system failures.

Key Takeaways

1. Software architecture is the high-level organizational and decision-making process for building software systems.

2. It aligns technical solutions with business needs, improves scalability, and reduces risk.

3. Good architecture focuses on clarity, modularity, and long-term goals, while poor architecture leads to inefficiency and technical debt.

Understanding these foundational concepts prepares learners to dive deeper into how software architecture shapes modern systems. The next lessons will explore the role of architects and the tangible value architecture brings to projects.

Lesson 1.2: The Role and Responsibilities of a Software Architect

A software architect is the bridge between technical teams and business stakeholders. The software architect is responsible for making critical decisions that shape the success of a software system. Their primary role is to ensure that the system's architecture aligns with both technical requirements and organizational goals, balancing the needs of the business with the constraints of technology.

Key Responsibilities of a Software Architect

1. **Defining the Architecture:**
    The architect designs the high-level structure of the system, outlining components, their interactions, and how they fulfill the system's requirements. This includes selecting architectural patterns (e.g., monolithic, distributed, micro-services) and technologies that best fit the project's needs.

2. **Ensuring Alignment with Business Goals:**
    A software architect works closely with stakeholders to translate business goals into technical solutions. They ensure the system supports current needs while remaining adaptable for future growth.

3. **Decision-Making:**
    Architects make critical decisions on tools, platforms, frameworks, and technologies, evaluating trade-offs

between performance, scalability, and cost. These decisions have long-lasting impacts on the project.

4. **Balancing Functional and Non-functional Requirements:**
   While developers focus on delivering features (functional requirements), the architect prioritizes non-functional requirements like performance, security, scalability, and maintainability.

5. **Technical Leadership and Mentorship:**
   Architects guide the development team by setting coding standards, providing technical expertise, and ensuring that implementation aligns with the architectural vision. They also mentor team members, helping them grow their technical skills.

6. **Risk Identification and Mitigation:**
   By anticipating potential risks—such as bottlenecks, scalability challenges, or security vulnerabilities—the architect mitigates issues before they become significant problems.

Technical and Soft Skills of a Software Architect

A software architect requires a mix of technical and interpersonal (soft) skills:

- **Technical Skills:** Deep knowledge of programming languages, frameworks, design patterns, and architectural styles. An architect should understand system design, DevOps practices, and cloud platforms.

- **Soft Skills:** Strong communication skills to collaborate with stakeholders, negotiate trade-offs, and lead teams effectively. Problem-solving and critical thinking skills are essential for making sound decisions under organizational and system constraints.

The Architect's Role in a Development Team

The architect acts as the **"technical guardian"** of the project, ensuring consistency across development, preventing scope creep, and maintaining a clear architectural vision. They bridge the gap between developers and non-technical stakeholders, translating complex technical details into actionable insights.

In essence, a software architect is a visionary, decision-maker, and mentor who ensures the system is efficient, scalable, and aligned with business objectives.

Analogy with Music Orchestra

In both music and software development, the conductor can be likened to a software architect. Just as the quality of an orchestra's performance hinges on the conductor's vision and leadership, the success of a software project depends on the architect. While individual musicians or developers play a vital role, it is the conductor or architect who envisions the final product and guides the team to bring it to life.

Influence of Stakeholders on The Architect

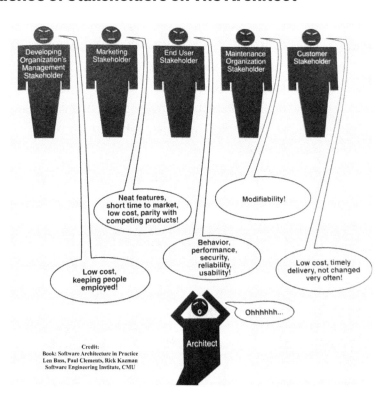

Credit:
Book: Software Architecture in Practice
Len Bass, Paul Clements, Rick Kazman
Software Engineering Institute, CMU

Lesson 1.3: The Value of Software Architecture in Projects

Software architecture is one of the most critical aspects of any software project, acting as a blueprint that guides development and ensures the system meets its objectives. A well-designed architecture brings significant value to a project, impacting everything from performance and scalability to maintainability and team productivity.

1. Enabling Scalability and Performance

Software systems must handle varying levels of user demand. A robust architecture ensures the system can scale effectively, whether that means adding more users, processing larger datasets, or integrating additional features. For example, a micro-services architecture allows individual services to scale independently, ensuring high performance under heavy loads.

Without careful architectural planning, systems often face bottlenecks that limit growth and frustrate users. A poorly designed system might work well with a few users but fail catastrophically under real-world conditions.

2. Improving Maintainability

Projects evolve over time, with new requirements, technologies, and constraints emerging. A good architecture makes systems easier to update and maintain by promoting modularity and separation of concerns. For instance, layered architecture separates business logic, data access, and user interfaces, simplifying updates or bug fixes without affecting unrelated parts of the system.

Without a maintainable architecture, developers face challenges such as tightly coupled components and undocumented dependencies, leading to increased development time and higher costs.

3. Addressing Non-Functional Requirements

While functional requirements (*features*) are the immediate focus of most projects, non-functional requirements like *security*, *reliability*, and *usability* often determine long-term success. Architecture ensures these requirements are integrated from the start. For example, fault-tolerant architectures can handle failures gracefully, ensuring system reliability.

4. Aligning Technical Solutions with Business Goals

Software architecture bridges the gap between technical implementation and business strategy. By understanding business objectives, architects design systems that not only meet technical requirements but also support growth, innovation, and competitive advantage.

5. Reducing Risks

Good architecture mitigates risks by identifying potential issues early in the project. It prevents technical debt, minimizes performance bottlenecks, and reduces the likelihood of costly redesigns or failures.

Key Takeaways

Investing in software architecture ensures scalability, maintainability, and alignment with business goals. It minimizes risks, improves developer productivity, and lays the foundation for long-term success. Ignoring architecture may save time initially but often leads to technical debt, increased costs, and project failures in the long run.

■■

CORE CONCEPTS AND TERMINOLOGY

Explores the essential concepts and terminology that form the foundation of software architecture. Understanding these core ideas is crucial for anyone looking to design, evaluate, or communicate about software systems effectively.

T his module begins with an introduction to architectural styles and patterns, which are reusable solutions to common system design problems. You will learn about key styles like monolithic, layered, client-server, and micro-services, exploring when and why to use each of them.

This module will also explain the key building blocks of software architecture: **components, connectors, and configurations**. Components represent the system's functional units, connectors define how components interact, and configurations describe how these pieces fit together. These concepts provide a clear framework for describing and analyzing any software architecture.

Additionally, this module covers functional and non-functional requirements. Functional requirements define the system's behavior, while non-functional requirements (e.g., performance, scalability, and security) address its quality attributes. Understanding how to balance and prioritize these requirements is a critical skill for architects.

By the end of this module, learners will have a solid grasp of the key terminology and concepts that underpin software architecture. This knowledge will serve as a foundation for exploring more advanced topics and enable effective communication with stakeholders, team members, and decision-makers.

With real-world examples, diagrams, and hands-on exercises, this module ensures a practical and accessible learning experience for both beginners and experienced professionals.

Lesson 2.1: Understanding Architectural Styles and Patterns

Architectural styles and patterns are foundational concepts in software architecture. They provide structured approaches to solving common system design challenges, ensuring scalability, maintainability, and efficiency.

What are Architectural Styles?

Architectural styles define the overarching structure of a system. They describe how components interact and the rules governing their organization. Some commonly used styles include:

1. **Monolithic Architecture:**
    - All components are tightly integrated into a single system.
    - Best for small applications with simple requirements.

    Example: Early versions of e-commerce platforms.

2. **Layered Architecture:**
    - The system is organized into layers, each with distinct responsibilities (e.g., presentation, business logic, data access).
    - Promotes separation of concerns and easier maintenance.

Example: Most web applications with Model-View-Controller (MVC) frameworks.

3. **Client-Server Architecture:**

   - Divides the system into clients (front-end) and servers (back-end).
   - Common in web and mobile applications.

   Example: Email systems.

4. **Microservices Architecture:**

   - Breaks the system into independent services that communicate via Application Programming Interfaces (APIs).
   - Enables scalability and independent deployment of services.

   Example: Netflix's streaming platform.

What are Architectural Patterns?

Patterns are reusable solutions for specific design problems. Unlike styles, which define overall system structure, patterns address specific challenges within that structure. Examples include:

1. **Model-View-Controller (MVC):**

   - Separates data (Model), user interface (View), and application logic (Controller).

   Example: Frameworks like Django or Ruby on Rails.

2. **Event-Driven Architecture:**

- Components respond to and handle events asynchronously.

    Example: Real-time applications like chat systems.

3. **Observer Pattern:**

- Allows one object to notify others of state changes.

    Example: Notifications in a weather app.

When to Use Styles and Patterns

Choosing the right style or pattern depends on the system's requirements, including scalability, performance, and maintainability. For instance, micro-services work well for complex, distributed systems, while layered architecture is ideal for simpler applications.

Key Takeaways

Architectural styles provide high-level organization, while patterns address specific problems. Together, they form a toolkit for designing efficient and maintainable systems. Understanding these concepts ensures that architects can build systems tailored to meet both technical and business needs.

Lesson 2.2: Components, Connectors, and Configurations Explained

The concepts of **components, connectors, and configurations** form the backbone of software architecture. They provide a structured way to describe and analyze how a system is organized, how its parts interact, and how it achieves its goals.

1. Components

Components are the fundamental building blocks of a system. They represent units of functionality or processing, such as modules, services, or libraries. Each component encapsulates a specific piece of the system's behavior and interacts with others to achieve the system's objectives.

Examples: A payment processor in an e-commerce system, a user authentication service, or a database manager.

Key Attributes:

- Clearly defined responsibilities.
- Encapsulation of data and functionality.
- Independence from other components, enabling modularity.

2. Connectors

Connectors define how components interact. They handle communication, coordination, and data transfer between components. Without connectors, components would be isolated and unable to work together.

Types of Connectors:

- **Procedure Call**: Functions or methods invoked between components.
- **Data Flow**: Streams of data passed between components.
- **Message Passing**: Communication via messages (e.g., in event-driven systems).

Example: In a web application, connectors include HTTP requests between the browser (client) and server.

3. Configurations

Configurations describe how components and connectors are arranged to form a complete system. They define the architecture's structure and specify relationships and dependencies.

Examples:

- A three-tier architecture: Presentation layer (UI), application layer (business logic), and database layer (data storage).
- A micro-services configuration with independent services connected via Representational State Transfer (REST or RESTFul) APIs.

Why These Concepts Matter

Understanding components, connectors, and configurations helps architects design systems that are modular, scalable, and maintainable. By focusing on these elements, learners can describe the architecture clearly, identify potential bottlenecks, and communicate effectively with stakeholders.

Key Takeaways

- **Components** represent functionality.
- **Connectors** enable communication.
- **Configurations** describe the system's structure.

Mastering these concepts will ensures that learners can design robust, efficient, and scalable software architectures.

Lesson 2.3: Functional vs. Non-functional Requirements in Architecture

In software architecture, requirements drive the design and structure of the system. These requirements are broadly categorized into **functional** and **non-functional requirements**, each playing a vital role in ensuring the system meets its objectives.

1. Functional Requirements

Functional requirements define **what the system does**—its core features and behavior. They describe specific actions or functions the system must perform to meet business needs.

Examples:

- User authentication and authorization.
- Processing payments in an e-commerce system.
- Retrieving and displaying user data on a dashboard.

Functional requirements are often documented as use cases, user stories, or system specifications. They are the "visible" aspects of the system that stakeholders directly interact with.

2. Non-functional Requirements (NFRs)

Non-functional requirements specify **how the system performs** its functions. They address quality attributes, operational constraints, and performance standards that the system must meet.

Examples:

- **Performance**: The system must handle 1,000 requests per second.
- **Scalability**: The system should support a growing number of users without degradation.
- **Security**: Data must be encrypted in transit and at rest.
- **Usability**: Interfaces should be user-friendly and accessible.

Unlike functional requirements, NFRs are often invisible to end users but critical to system success. Neglecting them can lead to poor user experiences, system failures, or security breaches.

Balancing Functional and Non-functional Requirements

Both types of requirements must work together. Functional requirements ensure the system delivers its core functionality, while non-functional requirements guarantee that it operates efficiently, securely, and reliably.

For example, a functional requirement may specify that a website allows users to search for products. An accompanying non-functional requirement might state that the search results must load within 2 seconds.

Key Takeaways

- **Functional requirements** define what the system does.

- **Non-functional requirements** define how the system performs.

Balancing these requirements is crucial for creating systems that are both feature-rich and high-quality. As a software architect, understanding and addressing both of these requirements ensures your designs meet user and business expectations effectively.

■■

SOFTWARE DEVELOPMENT LIFECYCLE AND ARCHITECTURE

Explores the relationship between the Software Development Lifecycle (SDLC) and software architecture, emphasizing how architecture guides and evolves throughout the lifecycle. It highlights the importance of integrating architectural thinking into each phase of software development to create systems that are robust, scalable, and aligned with business goals.

This module begins with an overview of the SDLC, covering its stages: **planning, design, development, testing, deployment, and maintenance.** Each stage has unique architectural considerations, such as defining system requirements during planning or ensuring architectural integrity during maintenance.

This module teaches how architectural decisions influence and are influenced by different development methodologies, such as **Waterfall, Agile,** and **DevOps.** For example, iterative approaches in Agile encourage architects to focus on incremental, flexible designs, while DevOps promotes automation and seamless integration between development and operations.

This module also emphasizes the iterative nature of architecture, which must adapt to changing requirements, technologies, and user needs. It will help learners understand the critical role of architects in maintaining a balance between short-term project goals and long-term system sustainability.

By the end of this module, learners will grasp how architecture underpins the entire development lifecycle and ensures that the software meets both functional and non-functional requirements at every stage. Practical insights and examples will illustrate how architects can proactively manage risks, foster collaboration, and drive the success of complex software projects.

Lesson 3.1: Differentiating Software Design and Software Architecture

Software architecture and software design are often confused; however, each serve a distinct purpose in software development. Understanding their differences is essential for creating robust, scalable systems.

What is Software Architecture?

Software architecture defines the **high-level structure** of a system. It focuses on key decisions that impact the system's scalability, performance, and maintainability. Architecture determines the overall blueprint, including the selection of architectural styles (e.g., monolithic, micro-services) and patterns (e.g., MVC, event-driven).

- **Scope**: System-wide; focuses on how components interact.
- **Objective**: Ensure the system meets non-functional requirements (e.g., scalability, reliability).

Example: Deciding to use a micro-services architecture for an e-commerce platform to handle high traffic.

What is Software Design?

Software design focuses on the **details of implementation** within components. It involves choosing algorithms, data structures, and coding practices for individual modules.

- **Scope**: Component or module-specific; focuses on internal logic.

- **Objective**: Implement functional requirements effectively and maintain code quality.

Example: Designing a caching algorithm for faster product searches in an e-commerce system.

Key Differences

1. **Level of Abstraction:** Architecture is high-level; design is detailed and low-level.

2. **Focus:** Architecture addresses "what" and "why"; design tackles "how."

3. **Purpose:** Architecture ensures system-wide goals; design ensures component functionality.

Why Both Matter

Architecture provides a roadmap, while design builds the system's features. Together, they create systems that are functional, scalable, and maintainable. Misalignment between the two can lead to inefficiencies, increased costs, or system failures.

Lesson 3.2: Software Development Methodologies Overview

Software development methodologies are structured approaches to organizing and managing the software development process. These methodologies impact how software architecture is designed, implemented, and evolved over time. Understanding their differences helps architects choose approaches that best align with project goals and constraints.

1. Waterfall Methodology

The Waterfall model is a linear, sequential approach where each phase of the Software Development Lifecycle (SDLC)—planning, design, development, testing, and deployment—must be completed before the next begins.

- **Strengths**: Clear structure, well-documented processes, easy to manage.
- **Limitations**: Inflexible to changes; costly to fix issues discovered in later stages.
- **Best for**: Projects with well-defined, stable requirements.

2. Agile Methodology

Agile emphasizes flexibility and iterative development. Work is divided into short cycles called sprints, with continuous delivery of small, functional increments.

- **Strengths**: Adapts to changing requirements, promotes collaboration, and delivers value early.
- **Limitations**: Requires close coordination and may lack predictability for large projects.
- **Best for**: Dynamic projects with evolving requirements.

3. DevOps Approach

DevOps integrates development and operations to streamline the delivery pipeline. It focuses on automation, continuous integration (CI), and continuous delivery (CD).

- **Strengths**: Accelerates delivery, improves quality through automation, and fosters collaboration.
- **Limitations**: Requires cultural and technical transformation, tools can be complex.
- **Best for:** Large-scale systems with frequent updates or deployments.

4. Lean and Kanban

Lean minimizes waste and focuses on delivering only what adds value, while Kanban visualizes workflow to improve efficiency.

- **Strengths**: Encourages incremental improvement and transparency.
- **Limitations**: Less prescriptive, requires teams to define workflows clearly.

- **Best for**: Optimizing workflows and reducing bottlenecks.

Key Takeaways

Each methodology impacts architectural decisions differently:

- **Waterfall** aligns with upfront architectural planning.
- **Agile** requires adaptive, incremental architecture.
- **DevOps** emphasizes automatable and flexible architectures.

Selecting the right methodology depends on factors like project scope, team size, and requirement stability. The goal is to ensure the methodology supports both technical and business objectives effectively.

Lesson 3.3: Iterative and Incremental Approaches in Architecture

Modern software development embraces **iterative and incremental approaches** to build systems in manageable steps, making architecture adaptable and resilient to change. These approaches balance delivering value early with maintaining a sustainable long-term design.

What is an Iterative Approach?

The iterative approach focuses on refining the architecture over multiple cycles. Instead of building the entire system upfront, smaller prototypes or versions are developed, tested, and improved based on feedback. Each iteration helps identify and fix architectural flaws, ensuring the system evolves to meet user needs.

- **Example**: In an e-commerce platform, the first iteration might include basic product browsing, with subsequent iterations adding features like a shopping cart and user reviews.
- **Benefits**: Continuous improvement, early detection of issues, and flexibility to adapt to changing requirements.

What is an Incremental Approach?

The incremental approach involves dividing the system into smaller, independent parts (increments). Each increment is fully developed, tested, and delivered as a functional unit.

These increments eventually integrate to form the complete system.

- **Example**: Developing an email system incrementally might involve first building the email sending feature, then adding inbox management and search functionality.
- **Benefits**: Faster delivery of functional pieces, reduced risk, and easier testing.

Applying Iterative and Incremental Approaches in Architecture

In architecture, these approaches allow architects to:

1. **Start Small:** Focus on core components or high-priority features first.

2. **Refine Continuously:** Use feedback loops to improve architectural decisions.

3. **Build in Chunks:** Deliver smaller parts that can scale and integrate seamlessly.

Challenges

- Requires balancing short-term goals (quick delivery) with long-term architectural integrity.
- Poor communication between iterations can lead to misaligned components.

Key Takeaways

The iterative approach refines architecture over time, while the incremental approach builds systems in functional pieces. Combining both allows architects to create adaptable, scalable systems that deliver value early while ensuring a solid foundation for future growth. These methods are essential in Agile and DevOps environments where flexibility and speed are priorities.

■■

BASIC ARCHITECTURAL STYLES AND PATTERNS

Introduces the foundational architectural styles and patterns that shape software systems. These styles and patterns provide reusable solutions to common design challenges, enabling architects to create systems that are scalable, maintainable, and aligned with business goals.

This module begins with an overview of **architectural styles**, which define the high-level organization of a system. Key styles include **monolithic architecture**, ideal for small, simple applications; **layered architecture**, which separates concerns for better maintainability; and **client-server architecture**, used for many web and mobile applications. Each style is explained with its strengths, weaknesses, and use cases.

Next, the module explores **architectural patterns**, which solve specific design problems within a given architectural style. Patterns like **Model-View-Controller (MVC)** organize user interface systems, while **event-driven architecture** handles real-time communication in distributed systems. Learners will understand how patterns like the **observer**

pattern and **dependency injection** enhance modularity and flexibility.

By the end of the module, learners will grasp how to select appropriate styles and patterns based on system requirements, trade-offs, and constraints. Practical examples and case studies illustrate how these approaches are applied in real-world projects. This module equips learners with a toolkit to structure software systems effectively, laying the groundwork for advanced architectural strategies in later modules.

Lesson 4.1: Monolithic Architecture: Strengths and Weaknesses

Monolithic architecture is one of the simplest and most widely used architectural styles. In a monolithic system, all components—such as the user interface, business logic, and database interactions—are tightly integrated into a single executable or deployable unit.

Strengths of Monolithic Architecture

1. **Simplicity in Development and Deployment:**
   Monolithic systems can be simple and straightforward to develop because all components reside in a single codebase. Deployment is easier since the entire system is packaged and deployed as one unit.

2. **Performance Benefits:**
   Communication between components happens within the same process, making it faster than inter-process communication in distributed systems.

3. **Ease of Testing:**
   With all components in one place, end-to-end testing is less complicated compared to distributed architectures.

4. **Lower Initial Costs:**
   Fewer resources are needed for managing and maintaining monolithic applications, making them suitable for small teams or startups.

Weaknesses of Monolithic Architecture

1. **Scalability Challenges:**
   Monolithic systems scale vertically (by adding resources to a single server), which is limited and costly compared to horizontal scaling (adding more servers) in distributed systems.

2. **Tightly Coupled Components:**
   Any change to one component often requires rebuilding and redeploying the entire system, leading to slower development cycles.

3. **Difficult Maintenance:**
   As the codebase grows, it becomes harder to manage. Developers may encounter **"spaghetti code"** where dependencies between components are unclear.

4. **Lack of Flexibility:**
   Technology choices are constrained because all components must use the same technology stack, even if some components could benefit from different tools.

5. **Risk of Failure:**
   A failure in one part of the system can bring down the entire application, as all components are interconnected.

When to Use Monolithic Architecture

Monolithic architecture is ideal for:

- Small to medium-sized applications.
- Projects with well-defined, stable requirements.
- Startups or small teams that need to move quickly without the complexity of distributed systems.

Key Takeaways

Monolithic architecture offers simplicity and performance benefits but struggles with scalability, flexibility, and maintainability as systems grow. While suitable for small projects, larger systems often require transitioning to more scalable architectures, such as micro-services.

Lesson 4.2: Layered Architecture: A Deeper Look

Layered architecture, also known as the **n-tier architecture**, organizes a software system into distinct layers, each with specific responsibilities. This separation of concerns simplifies development, testing, and maintenance by clearly defining boundaries between functionality.

Structure of Layered Architecture

A typical layered architecture includes the following layers:

1. **Presentation Layer:**

   - Handles the user interface and user interaction.

   Example: A web page or mobile app displaying data.

2. **Application/Business Logic Layer:**

   - Manages the system's core logic and workflows.

   Example: Calculating a user's order total in an e-commerce system.

3. **Data Access Layer:**

   - Provides access to databases or external data sources.

   Example: SQL queries fetching product data.

4. **Database Layer:**

   - Stores and retrieves persistent data.

   Example: MySQL or MongoDB database.

Strengths of Layered Architecture

1. **Separation of Concerns:**
    Each layer focuses on a specific role, making the system easier to understand, develop, and test.

2. **Modularity:**
    Layers can be developed, updated, or replaced independently without affecting other layers.

3. **Reusability:**
    Logic in one layer can be reused across multiple applications (e.g., a shared data access layer).

4. **Ease of Maintenance:**
    Changes in one layer (e.g., database updates) have minimal impact on others.

Weaknesses of Layered Architecture

1. **Performance Overhead:**
    Communication between layers adds latency, especially in systems with heavy data processing.

2. **Rigid Structure:**
    Enforcing strict boundaries can limit flexibility, especially for rapidly evolving systems.

3. **Complexity for Simple Applications:**
    For small projects, the overhead of managing multiple layers may outweigh the benefits.

When to Use Layered Architecture

Layered architecture works well for:

- Applications with clear boundaries between responsibilities (e.g., CRUD systems).
- Systems with requirements for scalability and maintainability.
- Teams with developers specializing in specific layers.

Key Takeaways

Layered architecture provides a clean, modular design that simplifies development and maintenance. While it introduces some performance overhead, its benefits in scalability and flexibility make it ideal for medium to large applications, such as enterprise web applications and RESTful APIs.

Lesson 4.3: Client-Server Architecture and Its Applications

Client-server architecture is a foundational software design paradigm where the system is divided into two primary entities: **clients** and **servers**. This architecture is widely used in web applications, mobile apps, and distributed systems.

How Client-Server Architecture Works

1. **Client:**

   - The client is the user-facing part of the system, responsible for sending requests to the server and presenting responses.

   Examples: Web browsers, mobile apps, or desktop software.

2. **Server:**

   - The server processes client requests, performs operations (e.g., data retrieval, computations), and returns responses.

   Examples: Web servers like Apache, application servers like Node.js, or database servers.

Communication occurs over a network, often using HTTP, TCP/IP, or WebSocket protocols. For instance, in a web application, the browser (client) requests a webpage, and the server sends the HTML, CSS, and data needed to render it.

Strengths of Client-Server Architecture

1. **Centralized Control:**
   Servers centralize data and application logic, simplifying updates and security management.

2. **Scalability:**
   Multiple clients can interact with a single server, making it easier to scale horizontally by adding more servers.

3. **Resource Sharing:**
   Clients access shared resources, such as databases, through the server.

Weaknesses of Client-Server Architecture

1. **Single Point of Failure:**
   If the server goes down, clients lose access to the system.

2. **Scalability Limitations:**
   Servers can become bottlenecks under heavy traffic if not designed to scale effectively.

3. **Latency:**
   Communication over networks introduces latency, especially in geographically distributed systems.

Applications of Client-Server Architecture

- **Web Applications:** Browsers (clients) interact with web servers to fetch and display content.

- **Email Systems:** Clients like Outlook or Gmail connect to email servers.

- **Banking Applications:** Users access accounts and perform transactions via client apps communicating with secure servers.

Key Takeaways

Client-server architecture is ideal for systems requiring centralized control and shared resources. While it faces challenges like server bottlenecks and latency, its flexibility and scalability make it a go-to solution for web applications, mobile systems, and distributed computing.

■■

INTRODUCTION TO QUALITY ATTRIBUTES

Explores **quality attributes**, which define how well a software system performs its tasks. While functional requirements specify what a system does, quality attributes address **non-functional requirements (NFRs)**, such as performance, scalability, security, and maintainability, which directly impact user satisfaction and system success.

This module begins by explaining the importance of quality attributes in software architecture. These attributes influence key decisions during the design phase, shaping how systems handle demands like large-scale traffic, data security, or fast response times.

Next, it categorizes quality attributes into two types:

1. **Runtime Attributes:** Attributes that manifest during system operation, such as performance, scalability, availability, and security.

2. **Design-time Attributes:** Attributes that impact system development and maintenance, such as modifiability, testability, and portability.

The module also discusses trade-offs between attributes, like optimizing for performance at the cost of maintainability. Architects must balance these trade-offs to meet business and user needs effectively.

Practical examples and case studies illustrate how focusing on quality attributes leads to robust and efficient systems. For instance, a system designed for high availability minimizes downtime and enhances user trust, while a focused on modifiability adapts easily to changing requirements, reduces long-term costs.

By the end of this module, learners will understand the role of quality attributes in shaping software architecture and be prepared to successfully integrate them into design decisions.

Lesson 5.1: What Are Quality Attributes?

Quality attributes are the non-functional characteristics of a software system that define how it performs, behaves, and adapts to various conditions. While functional requirements specify **what the system does**, quality attributes describe **how well** it does it. They are critical for determining the system's usability, reliability, scalability, and overall success.

Types of Quality Attributes

Quality attributes are broadly categorized into two groups:

Runtime Attributes:
These attributes influence the system's behavior during operation. Examples include:

- **Performance**: How quickly the system responds to user actions or processes tasks.
- **Scalability**: The system's ability to handle increased workload or users.
- **Availability**: The percentage of time the system is operational and accessible.
- **Security**: Protection of data and resources from unauthorized access or attacks.

Design-time Attributes:
These attributes impact the development, testing, and maintenance phases. Examples include:

- **Maintainability**: How easily the system can be updated or fixed.

- **Testability**: The ease of verifying that the system works as intended.
- **Portability**: The ability to adapt the system to different platforms or environments.

Why Quality Attributes Matter

Quality attributes are essential for aligning technical decisions with business goals and user expectations. For instance:

- A high-performing system improves user satisfaction and competitiveness.
- A secure and available system builds trust and reliability.
- Maintainable and testable systems reduce long-term development costs.

Balancing Trade-offs

Quality attributes often conflict with one another, requiring architects to prioritize based on the project's goals. For example, optimizing for performance might increase costs or reduce maintainability.

Key Takeaways

Quality attributes define how well a system achieves its goals and adapts to challenges. By understanding and prioritizing these attributes, architects can design systems that meet user needs, support business objectives, and ensure long-term success.

Lesson 5.2: Exploring Performance, Reliability, Scalability, Security, Availability, and Maintainability

Quality attributes like **performance, reliability, scalability, security, availability,** and **maintainability** are crucial for the success of a software system. Each attribute addresses a specific aspect of system quality, impacting how users experience and interact with the system.

1. Performance

Performance refers to how quickly and efficiently a system completes tasks. It includes response time, throughput, and resource utilization.

- **Example**: A website that loads in under 2 seconds enhances user satisfaction.
- **Key Metrics**: Latency, throughput, and CPU/memory usage.

Use Case Scenario:

A real-time stock trading platform processes millions of buy and sell orders daily. Traders depend on fast execution to capitalize on market opportunities, where even milliseconds can mean the difference between profit and loss.

Performance in a Real-Time Stock Trading Platform

Source:
A trader submitting a buy or sell order through the platform's web or mobile application.

Stimulus:
A surge in incoming orders due to a significant market event (e.g., a company's earnings report), resulting in a high volume of requests within a short period.

Artifact:
The trading platform's order processing system, including APIs, matching engine, and backend databases that store transaction records.

Environment:
The system is live in a production environment during peak trading hours, where high request volume and low latency are critical.

Response:
The system should process and confirm orders within 10 milliseconds, ensuring fair execution and market transparency. It must also handle the surge in requests without degradation in response time.

Response Measure:

- **Latency:** 95% of orders must be processed in under 10 milliseconds.
- **Throughput:** The system should handle up to 1 million transactions per second during peak load.

- **Scalability:** Automatically scale backend resources (e.g., servers, databases) to accommodate surges.
- **Error Rate:** The error rate during high load should remain under 0.01%.
- **Monitoring:** Continuous monitoring with alerts for latency spikes or processing delays.

This approach ensures the trading platform maintains high performance, delivering a seamless user experience even during extreme market conditions.

2. Reliability

Reliability measures the system's ability to operate without failures over time. It ensures users can depend on the system to work as expected.

- **Example**: A payment gateway that processes transactions without errors.
- **Key Practices**: Error handling, fault tolerance, and testing.

Use Case Scenario:

A healthcare management system is used by hospitals to manage patient records, schedule appointments, and process lab results. Doctors and nurses rely on the system to access critical patient data, and any system failure could disrupt patient care and result in severe consequences.

Reliability in a Healthcare Management System

Source:
A hospital staff member (e.g., a doctor or nurse) attempting to access a patient's medical record during a consultation.

Stimulus:
A hardware failure, unexpected software bug, or external dependency failure (e.g., third-party lab result APIs) disrupts system functionality.

Artifact:
The healthcare management system, including its database for patient records, API integrations, and user interfaces.

Environment:
The system is in production, actively being used during peak hours in a hospital setting, with multiple simultaneous users accessing and updating records.

Response:
The system should ensure continuity of operations by gracefully handling failures through redundancy, transaction retries, and fallback mechanisms.

Response Measure:

- **Error Recovery Rate:** The system should recover from 99.9% of failures within 5 seconds.
- **Data Integrity:** 100% consistency and accuracy of patient records must be maintained during recovery operations.

- **Uptime:** The system must provide 99.999% reliability, with a maximum allowable downtime of 5 minutes per year.

- **User Notification:** Meaningful feedback should be provided to users during interruptions, along with guidance for retrying actions.

- **Redundancy:** Active-passive failover mechanisms should ensure minimal disruption in case of hardware or software failures.

By emphasizing reliability, this healthcare management system ensures seamless access to patient data, even during unexpected failures, safeguarding patient care and maintaining trust among medical professionals.

3. Scalability

Scalability is the system's ability to handle increasing workloads by adding resources.

- **Example**: An e-commerce platform that supports peak holiday traffic.

- **Types**: Horizontal (adding servers) and vertical (adding resources to a single server).

Use Case Scenario:

A video streaming platform hosts thousands of movies and TV shows for millions of users worldwide. During the release of a highly anticipated show, traffic spikes significantly as users across multiple regions log in to watch simultaneously.

Scalability in a Video Streaming Platform

Source:
A user accessing the platform to stream the newly released episode during peak traffic hours.

Stimulus:
A sudden surge in concurrent users, increasing requests to stream videos, authenticate accounts, and serve personalized recommendations.

Artifact:
The video streaming system, including the content delivery network (CDN), user authentication service, recommendation engine, and video encoding/streaming servers.

Environment:
The system is live in production, experiencing a high load during a global release event.

Response:
The system should scale seamlessly to handle the increased load without impacting video quality, playback speed, or user experience. It must maintain low latency and high throughput across all services.

Response Measure:

- **Elasticity:** The system must auto-scale resources (e.g., servers, databases) to accommodate up to 5x the normal load within 30 seconds of detecting increased traffic.
- **Latency:** Video playback should start within 2 seconds for 99% of users.
- **Throughput:** The platform must handle up to 10 million simultaneous streams without degradation.
- **Error Rate:** Keep API and streaming errors under 0.1% during peak loads.
- **Regional Load Balancing:** Redirect user requests to the nearest, least-loaded CDN node to optimize performance.

By designing for scalability, the video streaming platform ensures smooth and reliable service during traffic surges, delivering an exceptional user experience even during global events.

4. Security

Security protects the system from unauthorized access, data breaches, and attacks.

- **Example**: Encrypted communication between clients and servers (e.g., HTTPS).
- **Practices**: Authentication, authorization, encryption, and regular vulnerability assessments.

Use Case Scenario:

An online banking platform allows users to manage accounts, transfer funds, and access sensitive financial information. Protecting user data and preventing unauthorized access are critical to maintaining customer trust and regulatory compliance.

Security in an Online Banking System

Source:
A malicious actor attempting to gain unauthorized access to a user's banking account through phishing or brute-force attacks.

Stimulus:
An unauthorized login attempt, data exfiltration attempt, or suspicious activity detected, such as multiple failed login attempts or accessing the system from unusual locations.

Artifact:
The online banking application, including its authentication service, database storing sensitive financial information, and APIs exposed for mobile and web clients.

Environment:
The system is live in a production environment, accessed by users via web and mobile applications, and exposed to potential external threats.

Response:

The system must block unauthorized access attempts, alert administrators, and log suspicious activities for investigation. If a threat compromises a session, the system should revoke access and initiate recovery protocols.

Response Measure:

- **Authentication Robustness:** Enforce multi-factor authentication (MFA) for all users, reducing the success of brute-force attacks.

- **Intrusion Detection:** Detect and block 99.99% of malicious activities within 1 second using AI-based threat detection.

- **Data Encryption:** All sensitive data (in transit and at rest) must be encrypted using strong protocols (e.g., TLS 1.3, AES-256).

- **User Notification:** Notify users of unusual login attempts and require additional verification.

- **Compliance:** Ensure compliance with financial regulations like PCI DSS and GDPR to avoid penalties and enhance trust.

By prioritizing security, the online banking system protects user assets, maintains data privacy, and ensures trustworthiness, even in the face of evolving cyber threats.

5. Availability

Availability ensures the system is operational and accessible when needed, typically measured as a percentage (e.g., "99.9% uptime").

- **Example**: A cloud service with minimal downtime ensures customer trust.
- **Key Practices:** Redundancy, failover mechanisms, and monitoring.

Use Case Scenario:

An online payment gateway processes transactions for an e-commerce platform. Customers rely on the system to complete purchases at any time of day. If the payment gateway becomes unavailable, transactions fail, leading to lost sales and customer dissatisfaction.

Availability in an Online Payment Gateway

Source:
The source is a customer attempting to make a payment on the e-commerce platform.

Stimulus:
A network failure, server crash, or overload of requests causes a disruption in the payment processing system.

Artifact:
The payment gateway application, which includes transaction processing services, databases, and external APIs (e.g., payment providers like Visa or PayPal).

Environment:
The system is live in a production environment, handling real-time transactions during peak traffic hours.

Response:
The system should maintain operational continuity by rerouting requests, recovering from failures, or notifying users of temporary unavailability with a retry mechanism.

Response Measure:

- **System Recovery Time Objective (RTO):** The system must recover within 1 second to prevent transaction failure.

- **Failover Success Rate:** 99.99% of requests should be successfully rerouted to a backup server or redundant payment service.

- **Uptime:** The system should achieve 99.999% availability over a month, ensuring minimal downtime.

- **User Feedback:** A meaningful error message should be displayed if recovery is delayed, with an option to retry.

This structured approach ensures a robust design capable of maintaining availability even in adverse conditions.

6. Maintainability

Maintainability defines how easily a system can be updated, fixed, or enhanced over time.

- **Example**: A modular application with clean code can be updated without breaking functionality.
- **Practices**: Documentation, code modularity, and automated testing.

Use Case Scenario:

An inventory management system tracks stock levels, orders, and shipments for a retail chain. As business requirements evolve, frequent updates are needed to add new features, fix bugs, and optimize performance without disrupting ongoing operations.

Maintainability in an Inventory Management System

Source:
A developer or DevOps engineer working on a new feature or bug fix for the inventory system.

Stimulus:
A request for changes, such as adding support for a new supplier API integration, modifying business rules, or fixing a performance bottleneck.

Artifact:
The inventory management application, including its codebase, API services, and database schemas.

Environment:
The system is in the development stage, undergoing updates while ensuring smooth integration with existing production workflows.

Response:
The system should allow developers to make updates with minimal effort, risk, and downtime. Changes should be implemented without affecting unrelated parts of the system.

Response Measure:

- **Modularity:** Ensure the codebase is modular and follows clean coding practices (e.g., SOLID principles) to enable easy updates.

- **Testing Coverage:** Maintain at least 90% unit test coverage to ensure changes don't introduce regressions.

- **Deployment Time:** Updates should be deployable to production within 10 minutes using CI/CD pipelines.

- **Downtime:** Zero-downtime deployment should be supported for critical updates, ensuring uninterrupted service.

- **Documentation:** All changes must include updated documentation, reducing onboarding time for new developers.

By designing for maintainability, the inventory management system allows efficient updates, ensures system reliability, and reduces long-term development costs, enabling the business to adapt quickly to new opportunities and challenges.

Key Takeaways

Balancing these attributes ensures that systems perform well, meet user expectations, and adapt to future demands. Architects must prioritize based on project needs and continuously evaluate trade-offs to achieve optimal results.

Lesson 5.3: Design Approaches for Performance, Reliability, Scalability, Security, Availability, and Maintainability

A. Design Approach for Performance

Achieving high performance in a system requires optimizing resource utilization and ensuring the system can handle varying loads efficiently. Below is a design approach considering **Resource Demand**, **Resource Management**, and **Resource Arbitration**, along with commonly used mechanisms for each.

1. Resource Demand

Managing the demand for resources effectively ensures that the system can handle peak loads without compromising performance.

Mechanisms:

(i) **Caching:**

- Store frequently accessed data in memory to reduce demand on databases or external APIs.

  Example: Use tools like Redis or Memcached to cache database query results or API responses.

(ii) **Load Distribution:**

- Distribute workloads evenly across available resources to avoid hotspots.

Example: Use load balancers (e.g., NGINX, AWS Elastic Load Balancer) to direct traffic to the least loaded server.

(iii) **Data Partitioning:**

- Split large datasets into smaller chunks to optimize query performance.

Example: Shard databases (e.g., MongoDB, MySQL) to distribute queries across multiple nodes.

(iv) **Asynchronous Processing:**

- Handle non-critical tasks asynchronously to reduce immediate resource demand.

Example: Use message queues like RabbitMQ or Kafka for delayed processing.

2. Resource Management

Efficient management of available resources ensures optimal utilization without over-provisioning or under-utilization.

Mechanisms:

(i) **Auto-Scaling:**

- Automatically adjust resources based on current load.

Example: AWS Auto Scaling or Kubernetes Horizontal Pod Autoscaler (HPA).

(ii) **Concurrency Control:**

- Limit the number of concurrent operations to prevent resource exhaustion.

Example: Use thread pools in backend servers to control simultaneous requests.

(iii) **Efficient Algorithms:**

- Optimize algorithms to reduce CPU, memory, or I/O demands.

Example: Use time-efficient sorting algorithms like quicksort instead of bubble sort for large datasets.

(iv) **Compression:**

- Compress data to reduce transmission time and storage space.

Example: Use Gzip for compressing HTTP responses or database storage.

3. Resource Arbitration

When resource contention occurs, prioritizing and allocating resources effectively ensures smooth system operation.

Mechanisms:

(i) **Priority Queuing:**

- Assign priorities to tasks or requests to ensure critical ones are handled first.

Example: Implement priority-based scheduling in API request handlers.

(ii) **Rate Limiting:**

- Throttle excessive requests to maintain fairness and prevent resource hogging.

Example: Use API Gateways like Kong or AWS API Gateway for request rate limiting.

(iii) **Fair Scheduling:**

- Allocate resources fairly among competing processes or users.

Example: Use container orchestrators like Kubernetes to ensure fair CPU and memory allocation across pods.

(iv) **Circuit Breakers:**

- Temporarily block requests to a service if it becomes overloaded.

Example: Use Hystrix to prevent resource contention in microservices.

Key Takeaways

By balancing resource demands, efficient management, and fair arbitration, systems can achieve high performance under various load conditions. Leveraging these mechanisms ensures scalability, responsiveness, and efficient utilization of available resources.

B. Design Approach for Reliability

Reliability ensures that a system performs its intended functions consistently over time, maintaining data integrity, uptime, and quick error recovery. A robust design approach should address **Data Integrity**, **Uptime**, **Error Recovery Rate**, **Redundancy**, and **User Notification**. Below is a detailed strategy with commonly used mechanisms.

1. Data Integrity

Ensuring the accuracy and consistency of data throughout its lifecycle is critical for reliability.

Mechanisms:

(i) **Transaction Management:**

- Use ACID-compliant databases to ensure atomicity, consistency, isolation, and durability of transactions.

    Example: PostgreSQL or MySQL for financial systems.

(ii) **Checksums and Hashing:**

- Validate data integrity during transmission or storage using checksums.

    Example: Use MD5 or SHA-256 hashing for verifying file integrity.

(iii) **Data Validation:**

- Implement strict validation rules for user inputs and system-generated data.

Example: Use schema validation in JSON or XML APIs.

(iv) **Audit Trails:**

- Record data changes to detect inconsistencies or unauthorized modifications.

Example: Maintain a change log table for sensitive data.

2. Uptime

Maximizing uptime ensures continuous service availability.

Mechanisms:

(i) **High-Availability Architectures:**

- Deploy redundant resources in active-active or active-passive configurations.

Example: Use AWS Multi-AZ deployments for databases.

(ii) **Load Balancers:**

- Distribute traffic to healthy instances and reroute away from failed ones.

Example: Use Elastic Load Balancer (ELB) or HAProxy.

(iii) **Service Monitoring and Alerts:**

- Continuously monitor system health and set up alerts for outages.

Example: Use Prometheus or Datadog for real-time monitoring.

3. Error Recovery Rate

Quickly recovering from errors minimizes disruption.

Mechanisms:

(i) **Failover Mechanisms:**

- Automatically switch to backup resources during failures.

Example: Use MySQL Replication with automatic failover tools.

(ii) **Retry Policies:**

- Retry failed operations with exponential backoff to handle transient issues.

Example: Implement retries in HTTP clients like Axios or Java's RestTemplate.

(iii) **Graceful Degradation:**

- Reduce functionality instead of failing entirely during an issue.

Example: Show cached results if the live database is unavailable.

4. Redundancy

Building redundancy prevents single points of failure.

Mechanisms:

(i) **Data Replication:**

- Maintain multiple copies of data across different nodes or regions.

Example: Use MongoDB Replica Sets or Amazon S3 Cross-Region Replication.

(ii) **Clustered Infrastructure:**

- Deploy applications in clusters for fault tolerance.

Example: Use Kubernetes clusters with redundant nodes.

(iii) **Backup Systems:**

- Regularly back up critical data and configurations.

Example: Schedule automated backups in AWS RDS or Google Cloud Storage.

5. User Notification

Communicating with users during incidents maintains trust.

Mechanisms:

(i) **Real-Time Notifications:**

- Notify users of outages, delays, or recovery status via email, SMS, or in-app messages.

Example: Use Twilio or AWS SNS for alerting.

(ii) **Status Pages:**

- Provide a public status page showing service availability and incident updates.

Example: Use Statuspage.io for hosted status pages.

(iii) **Fallback Messaging:**

- Show user-friendly error messages with guidance for next steps.

Example: Display "Service temporarily unavailable, please try again later."

Key Takeaways

A reliable system incorporates mechanisms for data integrity, high uptime, swift error recovery, redundancy, and effective user communication. By adopting this approach, systems can maintain trust, minimize downtime, and deliver consistent performance even under adverse conditions.

C. Design Approach for Scalability

Scalability ensures that a system can handle increasing workloads effectively by scaling resources, optimizing performance, and distributing traffic efficiently. Below is a comprehensive approach addressing **Elasticity**, **Latency and Throughput**, and **Load Balancing**, with commonly used mechanisms and insights.

1. Elasticity

Elasticity allows systems to scale resources dynamically, adapting to fluctuating demands.

Mechanisms:

(i) **Auto-Scaling:**

- Automatically increase or decrease resources (e.g., compute instances, containers) based on demand.

Example: Use AWS Auto Scaling or Kubernetes Horizontal Pod Autoscaler (HPA).

(ii) **Serverless Architectures:**

- Use serverless computing to scale functions automatically without provisioning infrastructure.

Example: AWS Lambda or Google Cloud Functions.

(iii) **Database Sharding:**

- Partition data into smaller, independent shards to distribute load across multiple database instances.

Example: Implement sharding in MongoDB or MySQL.

(iv) **Caching Layers:**

- Use distributed caching to reduce load on the database and backend services.

Example: Use Redis or Memcached for caching frequently accessed data.

2. Latency and Throughput

Optimizing latency (response time) and throughput (requests processed per second) ensures high performance under varying loads.

Mechanisms:

(i) **Content Delivery Networks (CDNs):**

- Distribute static assets (e.g., images, videos, scripts) across global servers to reduce latency.

Example: Use Cloudflare or Akamai for global content delivery.

(ii) **Asynchronous Processing:**

- Offload time-consuming tasks to background workers to improve frontend response times.

Example: Use message queues like RabbitMQ or Kafka for asynchronous workflows.

(iii) **Database Read Replicas:**

- Create read replicas for heavy read operations to distribute the load.

Example: Use read replicas in AWS RDS or Google Cloud SQL.

(iv) **Efficient Data Compression:**

- Compress data to reduce transmission time and bandwidth usage.

Example: Use Gzip compression for HTTP responses.

(v) **Optimization of Algorithms:**

- Refactor code to use efficient data structures and algorithms.

Example: Replace $O(n^2)$ operations with $O(n \log n)$ alternatives, such as quicksort over bubble sort.

3. Load Balancing

Load balancing distributes traffic evenly across resources, ensuring optimal utilization and preventing bottlenecks.

Mechanisms:

(i) **Application Load Balancers:**

- Distribute HTTP/HTTPS requests based on application-level rules.

Example: AWS Application Load Balancer or NGINX.

(ii) **DNS-Based Load Balancing:**

- Use DNS records to direct traffic to multiple regions or servers.

Example: AWS Route 53 or Google Cloud DNS.

(iii) **Global Traffic Management:**

- Direct users to the nearest data center based on geolocation to reduce latency.

Example: Use tools like Azure Traffic Manager.

(iv) **Sticky Sessions:**

- Maintain session consistency by directing users to the same backend instance during a session.

  Example: Configure sticky sessions in HAProxy or AWS Elastic Load Balancer.

(v) **Dynamic Load Balancers:**

- Automatically adapt balancing strategies based on resource health and real-time metrics.

  Example: Use Kubernetes Ingress Controllers for containerized applications.

4. Best Practices:

(i) **Design for Horizontal Scaling:**

- Prefer scaling out (adding more instances) over scaling up (adding more resources to a single instance).

(ii) **Monitor and Alert:**

- Use monitoring tools like Prometheus, Datadog, or CloudWatch to track latency, throughput, and scaling metrics.

(iii) **Failover Strategies:**

- Incorporate failover mechanisms to handle resource failures gracefully.

Key Takeaways

By combining elasticity, throughput optimization, and load balancing, systems can achieve seamless scalability, maintaining high performance and reliability under fluctuating workloads. These mechanisms ensure your architecture remains robust and adaptive, meeting the demands of modern, dynamic environments.

D. Design Approach for Security

Ensuring robust security requires a multi-faceted design approach that addresses **resisting attacks**, **detecting attacks**, **recovering from attacks**, and ensuring **compliance and notification**. Below is a detailed approach with commonly used mechanisms for each aspect.

1. Resisting Attacks

Preventing unauthorized access and mitigating vulnerabilities to resist potential attacks.

Mechanisms:

(i) **Authentication and Authorization:**

- Ensure robust user identity verification and access control.

Example: Use multi-factor authentication (MFA) and Role-Based Access Control (RBAC).

(ii) **Data Encryption:**

- Encrypt data both in transit and at rest to prevent unauthorized access.

Example: Use TLS (e.g., TLS 1.3) for communication and AES-256 for storage.

(iii) **Input Validation and Sanitization:**

- Prevent injection attacks by validating and sanitizing user inputs.

Example: Use frameworks like OWASP ESAPI for secure input handling.

(iv) **Firewalls and Intrusion Prevention Systems (IPS):**

- Block malicious traffic and prevent unauthorized access to the network.

Example: Use tools like AWS WAF or Palo Alto firewalls.

(v) **Zero-Trust Architecture:**

- Assume no component is trusted by default; enforce authentication and authorization for all interactions.

Example: Use solutions like Google BeyondCorp.

2. Detecting Attacks

Identifying security breaches in real-time to minimize damage.

Mechanisms:

(i) **Intrusion Detection Systems (IDS):**

- Monitor and detect suspicious activities in the network or application.

  Example: Use Snort or Suricata for real-time traffic analysis.

(ii) **Log Monitoring and Analysis:**

- Analyze logs for anomalies or unauthorized access attempts.

  Example: Use centralized log systems like ELK Stack or Splunk.

(iii) **Threat Intelligence:**

- Leverage threat intelligence feeds to stay informed about emerging threats.

  Example: Use ThreatConnect or Recorded Future.

(iv) **Anomaly Detection with Machine Learning:**

- Use AI/ML to detect unusual patterns that might indicate an attack.

  Example: AWS GuardDuty or Azure Sentinel for automated threat detection.

3. Recovering from an Attack

Minimizing impact and restoring normalcy after an attack.

Mechanisms:

(i) **Backup and Disaster Recovery:**

- Maintain regular backups and ensure quick recovery mechanisms.

Example: Use automated snapshots in AWS RDS or Google Cloud.

(ii) **Incident Response Plans:**

- Have a documented and rehearsed plan for handling security incidents.

Example: Conduct regular red team/blue team exercises.

(iii) **Data Integrity Verification:**

- Verify the integrity of critical data after a breach.

Example: Use hash-based verification for critical databases.

(iv) **Service Isolation:**

- Isolate compromised services to prevent further propagation.

Example: Use Kubernetes Network Policies to restrict communication.

4. Compliance and Notification

Ensuring compliance with regulations and notifying stakeholders promptly.

Mechanisms:

(i) **Compliance Frameworks:**

- Adhere to industry standards like GDPR, HIPAA, PCI DSS, and ISO 27001.

Example: Use tools like Vanta or Drata for automated compliance checks.

(ii) **Automated Notifications:**

- Notify stakeholders and regulators promptly in case of a breach.

Example: Set up automated alerts with PagerDuty or Slack integrations.

(iii) **Audit Trails:**

- Maintain detailed logs for auditing purposes and regulatory compliance.

Example: Enable AWS CloudTrail or Azure Monitor for tracking system changes.

(iv) **User Education:**

- Regularly educate users on security best practices to prevent phishing and social engineering attacks.

Example: Conduct phishing simulations with tools like KnowBe4.

Key Takeaways

By implementing mechanisms for resisting, detecting, and recovering from attacks, alongside ensuring compliance, a secure system can be designed to protect sensitive data, maintain user trust, and meet regulatory requirements.

E. Design Approach for Availability

To achieve high availability in a system, it is essential to address faults proactively and reactively through a well-structured design approach. Below are key considerations and commonly used mechanisms for each stage:

1. Fault Detection

Fault detection involves identifying issues as soon as they occur to minimize downtime.

Mechanisms:

(i) **Health Checks:**

- Regularly monitor the health of services using tools like Kubernetes probes or AWS CloudWatch.

  Example: Liveness and readiness probes in Kubernetes to detect if a pod is functioning and ready to serve traffic.

(ii) **Heartbeat Signals:**

- Periodically send and monitor "heartbeat" messages between system components to detect failures.

Example: Distributed systems like Apache Kafka use ZooKeeper for heartbeat monitoring.

(iii) **Log Monitoring and Alerts:**

- Use logging and monitoring tools (e.g., ELK Stack, Splunk) to detect unusual patterns or errors.

Example: Set up alerts for a sudden increase in error rates or latency.

2. Recovery-Preparation and Repair

This stage involves preparing the system to handle faults and repairing any issues quickly.

Mechanisms:

(i) **Failover Systems:**

- Use active-passive or active-active failover configurations to switch to a backup system automatically.

Example: AWS Elastic Load Balancer routes traffic to healthy instances.

(ii) **Redundancy:**

- Maintain multiple instances of critical components to avoid single points of failure.

Example: Deploy replicas of databases using clustering (e.g., MySQL Cluster, MongoDB Replica Set).

(iii) **Backup and Restore:**

- Regularly back up data and have automated recovery mechanisms.

Example: Automated database snapshots in AWS RDS.

3. Recovery-Reintroduction

After recovering from a failure, reintroducing the repaired components into the system must be seamless.

Mechanisms:

(i) **Graceful Reintroduction:**

- Gradually reintroduce recovered services to production using canary or blue-green deployments.

Example: Use tools like Istio to manage traffic to reintroduced services incrementally.

(ii) **State Synchronization:**

- Synchronize the state between components to ensure consistency.

Example: Distributed caches like Redis or Hazelcast replicate state changes across nodes.

4. Prevention

Prevention focuses on minimizing the likelihood of faults occurring.

Mechanisms:

(i) **Load Balancing:**

- Distribute traffic evenly across resources to prevent overloads.

Example: Use load balancers like NGINX, HAProxy, or AWS Elastic Load Balancer.

(ii) **Rate Limiting and Throttling:**

- Limit the number of requests per user or service to prevent system strain.

Example: Implement API Gateway throttling to manage client requests.

(iii) **Chaos Engineering:**

- Intentionally inject failures into the system to identify weak points and improve resilience.

Example: Netflix's Chaos Monkey simulates failures to test availability under adverse conditions.

Key Takeaways

By incorporating mechanisms for fault detection, recovery, and prevention, systems can achieve high availability, ensuring minimal downtime and seamless user experiences even under adverse conditions.

F. Design Approach for Maintainability

To ensure a maintainable system, the design must accommodate **localized changes**, minimize **ripple effects**, support **deferred binding**, provide **uninterrupted service**, and enable **rapid deployability**. Below is a structured approach with commonly used mechanisms.

1. Localizing Change

Localizing changes ensures modifications can be made in a specific area without impacting the entire system.

Mechanisms:

(i) **Modular Design:**

- Break the system into independent, loosely coupled modules.

  Example: Implement layered architecture (e.g., presentation, business, data layers).

(ii) **Microservices Architecture:**

- Divide the application into independent microservices with clear boundaries.

Example: Separate order management, user authentication, and payment services.

(iii) **Encapsulation:**

- Hide implementation details within components, exposing only necessary interfaces.

Example: Use object-oriented principles like classes and interfaces.

2. Prevention of Ripple Effects

Avoid unintended consequences of changes in one module affecting others.

Mechanisms:

(i) **Dependency Injection:**

- Decouple components to reduce hard dependencies.

Example: Use Spring Framework or Guice in Java applications.

(ii) **Interface-Driven Design:**

- Use interfaces or abstract classes to define contracts, minimizing dependency on implementation.

Example: Define a PaymentProcessor interface with multiple implementations for various payment methods.

(iii) **Testing Automation:**

- Detect issues early with extensive unit, integration, and regression tests.

Example: Use tools like JUnit or pytest for automated testing pipelines.

3. Defer Binding Time

Allow certain decisions or configurations to be made later to accommodate changing requirements.

Mechanisms:

(i) **Configuration Management:**

- Externalize configurations to files or environment variables.

Example: Use .env files with frameworks like Spring Boot or dotenv in Node.js.

(ii) **Feature Toggles:**

- Enable or disable features dynamically without redeploying.

Example: Use LaunchDarkly for feature flag management.

(iii) **Dynamic Dependency Injection:**

- Load dependencies at runtime based on configuration.

Example: Use Java reflection or dynamic module loading in Python.

4. Uninterrupted Service

Ensure services remain available during updates or changes.

Mechanisms:

(i) **Blue-Green Deployment:**

- Deploy changes to a new environment (blue) while the old one (green) remains active, then switch traffic.

Example: AWS Elastic Beanstalk supports blue-green deployment natively.

(ii) **Rolling Updates:**

- Gradually update instances without taking the entire system offline.

Example: Use Kubernetes rolling updates for containerized applications.

5. Deployability in No Time

Enable rapid, error-free deployment of changes.

Mechanisms:

(i) **Continuous Integration/Continuous Delivery (CI/ CD):**

- Automate build, test, and deployment pipelines.

Example: Use Jenkins, GitHub Actions, or GitLab CI/CD.

(ii) **Immutable Infrastructure:**

- Deploy new instances instead of modifying existing ones.

Example: Use Docker images and container orchestration with Kubernetes.

(iii) **Package Managers:**

- Bundle and version components for easy deployment.

Example: Use Maven for Java or npm for Node.js.

Key Takeaways

By designing for localized change, ripple prevention, deferred binding, uninterrupted service, and rapid deployability, maintainability becomes an inherent quality of the system. These mechanisms ensure easier updates, reduced downtime, and long-term cost savings.

Lesson 5.4: Understanding Trade-offs in Architectural Decision-Making

Architectural decisions often involve making trade-offs to balance conflicting priorities. A trade-off is a compromise in which the improvement of one quality attribute may negatively impact another. Architects must evaluate these trade-offs to meet both technical and business goals effectively.

Why Trade-offs Are Necessary

Software systems cannot optimize every quality attribute simultaneously. For example:

- Improving performance may increase complexity, reducing maintainability.
- Enhancing security might require additional processing, impacting performance.
- Increasing scalability often leads to higher costs or reduced simplicity.

Trade-offs arise because resources like time, budget, and computing power are finite, and project requirements often conflict.

Common Trade-off Scenarios

1. **Performance vs. Maintainability:**
   Optimizing performance with low-level optimizations or complex algorithms can make code harder to understand and maintain.

Example: A gaming engine prioritizing speed over simplicity.

2. **Scalability vs. Cost:**
   Designing for scalability with distributed systems adds costs in terms of infrastructure and complexity.

   Example: Moving from a monolithic to a micro-services architecture.

3. **Security vs. Usability:**
   Strengthening security with multi-factor authentication may make the system less convenient for users.

   Example: A banking app requiring extra authentication steps.

4. **Availability vs. Consistency:**
   In distributed systems, maintaining availability during network partitions might sacrifice data consistency (e.g., in eventual consistency models).

   Example: Real-time messaging apps like WhatsApp prioritize availability.

How to Make Trade-offs

1. **Prioritize Requirements:**
   Focus on the most critical attributes based on business goals and user needs.

   Example: A financial app prioritizing security over speed.

2. **Analyze Impact:**
   Use tools like decision matrices or cost-benefit analyses to evaluate trade-offs.

3. **Iterate and Adapt:**
   Continuously reassess trade-offs as requirements evolve or new technologies emerge.

Key Takeaways

Trade-offs are inevitable in architectural decision-making. A well-balanced system considers both short-term needs and long-term sustainability, ensuring the most important attributes align with project objectives. Skilled architects make informed trade-offs to deliver systems that meet user expectations and business goals effectively.

■■

ARCHITECTURAL PATTERNS AND STYLES

Delves into **architectural patterns and styles**, providing reusable solutions for designing software systems. These patterns and styles serve as blueprints to address common challenges in software architecture, enabling the creation of systems that are scalable, maintainable, and robust.

The module begins with an exploration of **architectural styles**, which define the high-level organization of a system. Key styles include **event-driven architecture**, which excels in handling asynchronous workflows, and **service-oriented architecture (SOA)**, designed for distributed, modular systems. You will learn how these styles influence communication between components, resource management, and scalability.

Next, the module focuses on **architectural patterns**, which provide solutions to specific design problems. Patterns like **Model-View-Controller (MVC)** help separate concerns in user interface systems, while **CQRS (Command and Query Responsibility Segregation)** is ideal for systems requiring high performance and scalability in read and write operations. The module explains when and how to use these patterns effectively.

By the end of this module, learners will understand how to evaluate and apply architectural styles and patterns based on system requirements, constraints, and goals. Real-world examples and case studies will illustrate how these strategies solve complex design challenges in various domains, from enterprise applications to real-time systems. This module equips learners with the tools to design architectures that are both efficient and aligned with business needs.

Lesson 6.1: Event-Driven Architecture Basics

Event-driven architecture (EDA) is a design paradigm where components interact by producing and responding to events. It is highly flexible and well-suited for systems requiring real-time responsiveness, scalability, and decoupled communication.

How Event-Driven Architecture Works

In an EDA system:

1. **Event Producers** generate events. These are actions or changes that occur in the system, such as a user clicking a button, a payment being completed, or a sensor detecting temperature changes.

2. **Event Consumers** listen for and respond to these events by executing specific actions. For example, after a payment is processed, an event might trigger sending a receipt to the user.

3. **Event Channels/Brokers** handle the transmission of events between producers and consumers. Examples include message queues (e.g., RabbitMQ, Kafka) or pub/sub systems (e.g., AWS SNS).

Advantages of Event-Driven Architecture

1. **Decoupling:** Producers and consumers don't need to know about each other. This improves modularity and simplifies maintenance.

2. **Scalability:** Events can be processed asynchronously and distributed across multiple consumers, supporting large-scale systems.

3. **Real-Time Responsiveness:** EDA supports real-time use cases, such as IoT systems or live data streams.

4. **Flexibility:** Adding new features is easier by introducing new consumers without modifying existing components.

Challenges of Event-Driven Architecture

1. **Complexity:** Managing event flow, error handling, and debugging can be challenging.

2. **Consistency:** In distributed systems, ensuring data consistency across consumers requires careful planning.

3. **Latency:** High event traffic can introduce delays if not managed properly.

When to Use EDA

EDA is ideal for:

- Real-time systems (e.g., stock trading platforms, IoT networks).
- Distributed systems with asynchronous workflows (e.g., order processing in e-commerce).
- Applications requiring high decoupling and scalability.

Key Takeaways

Event-driven architecture enables scalable, decoupled, and real-time systems by leveraging events as a core communication mechanism. While it introduces complexity, its benefits make it invaluable for dynamic and distributed applications.

Lesson 6.2: Introduction to Microservices Architecture

Micro-services architecture is a design approach where an application is built as a collection of small, independent services that communicate through APIs. Each service focuses on a specific business capability, allowing teams to build, deploy, and scale components independently.

Core Principles of Micro-services Architecture

1. **Decoupling:**
    Services are loosely coupled, meaning changes in one service typically don't affect others.

    Example: An e-commerce app might have separate services for user management, inventory, and payment processing.

2. **Single Responsibility:**
    Each service is designed to perform one business function, such as handling orders or managing user authentication.

3. **API Communication:**
    Services interact using lightweight protocols like HTTP/REST or messaging systems like Kafka.

4. **Independent Deployment:**
    Services can be deployed, updated, and scaled independently, reducing downtime and improving agility.

Advantages of Micro-services Architecture

1. **Scalability:**
   Individual services can be scaled based on their specific demands (e.g., scaling the search service for high user queries).

2. **Fault Isolation:**
   A failure in one service does not bring down the entire system.

3. **Technology Flexibility:**
   Different services can use different programming languages or databases, tailored to their needs.

4. **Faster Development:**
   Independent teams can work on separate services simultaneously, speeding up delivery.

Challenges of Micro-services Architecture

1. **Increased Complexity:**
   Managing multiple services, their dependencies, and communication requires robust infrastructure.

2. **Network Overhead:**
   Communication between services over the network adds latency and requires careful design.

3. **Data Consistency:**
   Maintaining consistency across services in distributed systems is challenging.

4. **Monitoring and Debugging:**
    Identifying issues in a system with many services can be complex without proper tools.

When to Use Micro-services

Micro-services are ideal for:

- Large, complex systems requiring high scalability (e.g., Netflix, Amazon).
- Applications with distinct, modular business domains.
- Organizations with teams that can manage services independently.

Key Takeaways

Micro-services architecture promotes agility, scalability, and resilience by breaking down systems into small, manageable services. While it adds complexity, its benefits make it a preferred choice for modern, large-scale applications.

Lesson 6.3: Service-Oriented Architecture (SOA): Principles and Applications

Service-Oriented Architecture (SOA) is a design paradigm that structures software as a collection of **services**. These services represent reusable business functionalities that interact via well-defined protocols, often over a network. SOA enables modularity and reusability, making it a popular choice for enterprise systems.

Core Principles of SOA

1. **Service Abstraction:**
   Services hide their implementation details and expose only necessary interfaces for interaction.

2. **Loose Coupling:**
   Services are independent, reducing interdependencies and enabling flexibility in updates or changes.

3. **Reusability:**
   Services are designed to be reused across different applications or business processes.

4. **Interoperability:**
   SOA supports communication across heterogeneous systems using standard protocols like SOAP or REST.

5. **Discoverability:**
   Services are registered and can be dynamically discovered and used by other components.

Applications of SOA

1. **Enterprise Systems Integration:**
   SOA connects legacy systems, databases, and new applications, enabling seamless data exchange.

   Example: An airline system integrating booking, check-in, and loyalty management services.

2. **Business Process Automation:**
   SOA orchestrates reusable services to streamline workflows, such as order processing in retail.

3. **Cross-Platform Compatibility:**
   Services built in different technologies communicate efficiently using SOA.

Advantages of SOA

1. **Modularity:**
   Promotes easier updates, maintenance, and scalability.

2. **Reusability:**
   Reduces duplication by reusing services across applications.

3. **Scalability and Flexibility:**
   Independent services can scale or evolve without disrupting others.

Challenges of SOA

1. **Complexity:**
    Setting up and managing an SOA infrastructure requires significant planning and resources.

2. **Performance Overhead:**
    Network communication between services can add latency.

3. **Governance:**
    SOA demands strict governance to ensure service quality, version control, and security.

Key Takeaways

SOA organizes software as modular, reusable services, making it a powerful solution for enterprise integration and automation. While it introduces complexity, its benefits in flexibility, scalability, and interoperability make it ideal for large, distributed systems.

■■

DESIGN PATTERNS FOR ARCHITECTS

Delves into **design patterns**, proven solutions to recurring design problems in software architecture. These patterns provide architects with a toolkit to create robust, maintainable, and scalable systems by addressing common challenges in software development.

The module begins with an introduction to the importance of design patterns, emphasizing how they promote reusable and consistent designs. By understanding and applying these patterns, architects can simplify development, reduce technical debt, and enhance team productivity.

Next, the module explores key categories of design patterns:

1. **Creational Patterns:**
   Focus on object creation mechanisms, ensuring flexibility and scalability. Examples include the **Singleton**, **Factory**, and **Builder** patterns.

2. **Structural Patterns:**
   Deal with object composition, simplifying complex

relationships. Examples include **Adapter**, **Proxy**, and **Decorator** patterns.

3. **Behavioral Patterns:**
   Address object interactions and communication. Examples include **Observer**, **Strategy**, and **Command** patterns.

Each lesson dives into these patterns, explaining their purpose, structure, and real-world applications. For example, the **Observer pattern** is ideal for event-driven architectures, while the **Decorator pattern** adds dynamic functionality to objects.

By the end of the module, learners will understand how to select and implement the right design patterns to address architectural challenges. Through practical examples and case studies, this module equips architects with the skills to create well-structured, reusable, and maintainable systems, ensuring long-term success.

Lesson 7.1: Key Creational Design Patterns (Singleton, Factory, Builder)

Creational design patterns focus on optimizing **object creation** processes to improve flexibility, scalability, and code maintainability. Here we will explore three key creational patterns: **Singleton, Factory,** and **Builder**.

1. Singleton Pattern

The Singleton pattern ensures that a class has only **one instance** throughout its lifecycle and provides a global access point to it.

- **Use Case**: Ideal for managing shared resources, such as a configuration manager, database connection, or logging service.

Example: using Java programming language

```java
public class Singleton {
    private static Singleton instance;
    private Singleton() {}
    // Private constructor

    public static Singleton getInstance() {
        if (instance == null) {
            instance = new Singleton();
        }
        return instance;
    }
}
```

Benefits: Controls resource usage, ensures consistency.

Challenges: Can introduce bottlenecks in multi-threaded environments if not implemented carefully.

2. Factory Pattern

The Factory pattern provides a method to create objects **without specifying their exact class**, promoting flexibility and scalability.

- **Use Case:** When a system needs to create objects dynamically based on input or configuration.

Example: using Java programming language

```
interface Shape { void draw(); }
class Circle implements Shape {
    public void draw() {
        System.out.println("Circle");
    }
}
class Square implements Shape {
    public void draw() {
        System.out.println("Square");
    }
}
class ShapeFactory {
    public static Shape createShape(String type) {
        if ("circle".equalsIgnoreCase(type))
            return new Circle();
        else if ("square".equalsIgnoreCase(type))
            return new Square();
        return null;
    }
}
```

Benefits: Simplifies object creation, centralizes logic.

Challenges: Complex factories may require maintenance.

3. Builder Pattern

The Builder pattern simplifies the construction of **complex objects** by separating their creation process into multiple steps.

- **Use Case**: Useful when creating objects with many optional parameters.

Example: using Java programming language

```
public class Car {
    private String engine;
    private int wheels;
    public static class Builder {
        private String engine;
        private int wheels;
        public Builder setEngine(String engine) {
            this.engine = engine;
            return this;
        }
        public Builder setWheels(int wheels) {
            this.wheels = wheels;
            return this;
        }
        public Car build() {
            return new Car(this);
        }
    }
```

```
private Car(Builder builder) {
        this.engine = builder.engine;
        this.wheels = builder.wheels;
    }
}
```

Benefits: Improves readability and reduces errors in complex object creation.

Key Takeaways

- **Singleton**: Ensures one shared instance.

- **Factory**: Creates objects flexibly.

- **Builder**: Handles complex object construction step-by-step.

Understanding these patterns helps architects design flexible, scalable systems while minimizing redundancy and errors.

Lesson 7.2: Key Structural Design Patterns (Adapter, Proxy, Decorator)

Structural design patterns focus on **object composition** and define how classes and objects interact to form larger, more functional systems. Here, we will explore three essential structural patterns: **Adapter, Proxy,** and **Decorator.**

1. Adapter Pattern

The Adapter pattern acts as a **bridge** between two incompatible interfaces, allowing them to work together. It converts one interface into another without altering the existing code.

- **Use Case**: When integrating a third-party library or legacy system with an existing system.

Example: using Java programming language

```
interface Target {
    void request();
}
class Adaptee {
    void specificRequest(){
      System.out.println("Specific Request");
    }
}
class Adapter implements Target {
    private Adaptee adaptee;
    public Adapter(Adaptee adaptee) {
          this.adaptee = adaptee;
    }
```

```
    public void request() {
            adaptee.specificRequest();
    }
}
```

Benefits: Enables compatibility without changing existing classes.

Challenges: Overuse can add unnecessary complexity.

2. Proxy Pattern

The Proxy pattern provides a **substitute or placeholder** for another object to control access, enhance functionality, or add security.

- **Use Case:** Adding caching, lazy initialization, or access control.

Example: using Java programming language

```
interface Service {
    void execute();
}
class RealService implements Service {
    public void execute() {
        System.out.println("Executing Real Service");
    }
}
class ProxyService implements Service {
    private RealService realService;
    public void execute()
    {
        if (realService == null)
```

```
            realService = new RealService();
        System.out.println("Proxy Before Execution");
        realService.execute();
        System.out.println("Proxy After Execution");
    }
}
```

Benefits: Adds control, logging, or lazy loading without modifying the original class.

Challenges: Can introduce latency or complexity.

3. Decorator Pattern

The Decorator pattern **dynamically extends functionality** of an object without modifying its code.

- **Use Case**: Adding features to UI elements or logging functionality.

Example: using Java programming language

```
interface Component {
    void operation();
}
class ConcreteComponent implements Component {
    public void operation() {
        System.out.println("Core Functionality");
    }
}
class Decorator implements Component {
    private Component component;
    public Decorator(Component component) {
            this.component = component;
    }
```

```java
public void operation() {
    component.operation();
    System.out.println("Additional Functionality");
}
}
```

Benefits: Flexibility to add/remove features at runtime.

Challenges: Overuse can lead to complex hierarchies.

Key Takeaways

- **Adapter**: Bridges incompatible interfaces.

- **Proxy**: Controls access or adds enhancements.

- **Decorator**: Dynamically extends functionality.

These patterns improve flexibility, reuse, and functionality while maintaining clean, modular code.

Lesson 7.3: Key Behavioral Design Patterns (Observer, Strategy, Command)

Behavioral design patterns focus on how objects interact and communicate, enabling flexibility and reducing coupling in software systems. Three widely used behavioral patterns—**Observer, Strategy,** and **Command**—address common challenges in software architecture.

1. Observer Pattern

The Observer pattern establishes a **one-to-many dependency**, where multiple objects (observers) are notified automatically when the state of another object (subject) changes.

- **Use Case:** Real-time updates, such as notifying a UI component when data changes.

  Example: In a stock market application, multiple dashboards (observers) update when the stock price (subject) changes.

- **Implementation:**
  - ▶ The subject maintains a list of observers and notifies them of state changes.
  - ▶ Observers subscribe/unsubscribe dynamically.

- **Benefits:** Promotes decoupling between subjects and observers.

- **Challenges:** May lead to performance issues with many observers.

2. Strategy Pattern

The Strategy pattern allows you to **dynamically switch between algorithms** or behaviors at runtime by encapsulating them in separate classes.

- **Use Case**: When you need multiple algorithms for the same task, such as sorting strategies (bubble sort, quicksort).

- **Example**: A payment system where different payment methods (credit card, PayPal) are implemented as strategies.

- **Implementation**:
  - ► Define a common interface for all strategies.
  - ► The client chooses a strategy dynamically.

- **Benefits**: Promotes flexibility and adherence to the open/closed principle.

- **Challenges**: May increase complexity with many strategies.

3. Command Pattern

The Command pattern encapsulates **a request as an object**, allowing you to parameterize methods, delay execution, or log operations.

- **Use Case**: Undo/redo functionality, task queues, or remote control systems.

- **Example**: In a text editor, commands like "copy," "paste," and "undo" are encapsulated and executed later.

- **Implementation**:

  - ▶ The command object includes details of the request and knows how to execute it.

  - ▶ The invoker (e.g., a UI button) calls the command.

- **Benefits**: Decouples objects issuing requests from those executing them. Enables operation queuing or undo features.

- **Challenges:** Adds complexity with many command objects.

Key Takeaways

- **Observer:** Notifies dependents of changes automatically.

- **Strategy:** Dynamically switches between behaviors or algorithms.

- **Command:** Encapsulates requests for flexible execution.

These patterns enhance reusability, flexibility, and maintainability in system design, making them essential for solving behavioral challenges in architecture.

Lesson 7.4: Applying Design Patterns in Architectural Contexts

Design patterns play a crucial role in software architecture by providing reusable solutions to common problems. Applying them effectively in an architectural context ensures systems are scalable, maintainable, and aligned with both technical and business goals. Let's explore how key design patterns integrate into architectural decisions.

1. Leveraging Patterns for Scalability

Design patterns such as **Proxy** and **Singleton** help manage scalability in large systems:

- **Proxy Pattern**: Often used in distributed systems to implement caching or load balancing. For example, a proxy can cache frequently accessed data, reducing the load on a database.

- **Singleton Pattern**: Ensures a single instance of critical resources like configuration managers, enabling consistent behavior across distributed nodes.

2. Improving Modularity and Flexibility

Patterns like **Decorator** and **Factory** contribute to modular designs that adapt to changing requirements:

- **Decorator Pattern**: Adds functionality dynamically. For instance, in a UI system, decorators can apply themes or logging features without altering core components.

- **Factory Pattern**: Simplifies object creation. For example, in a micro-services architecture, factories create service instances based on runtime configurations.

3. Enhancing Maintainability

Patterns like **Observer** and **Adapter** streamline integration and maintenance:

- **Observer Pattern**: Ideal for event-driven architectures where one change triggers updates in dependent systems, such as updating UI components when backend data changes.

- **Adapter Pattern**: Bridges legacy systems with modern architectures, enabling phased migrations without disrupting existing functionality.

4. Solving Domain-Specific Challenges

Architectural styles like micro-services, event-driven systems, or RESTful APIs frequently use patterns to address domain challenges:

- In **event-driven** architectures, the **Command** pattern separates commands and queries for better scalability and maintainability.

- In **RESTful APIs**, the **Builder** pattern simplifies constructing complex query strings.

Key Takeaways

Applying design patterns in architectural contexts enhances system **scalability**, **flexibility**, and **maintainability**. Architects must select patterns based on project requirements, balancing simplicity and extensibility. When used effectively, patterns provide a blueprint for solving recurring problems, reducing complexity, and ensuring long-term system success.

■■

CHAPTER 8 (MODULE 8)

ARCHITECTURAL DOCUMENTATION AND COMMUNICATION

Delves into the critical skills of documenting and communicating software architecture. Effective documentation and communication bridge the gap between architects, developers, and stakeholders, ensuring alignment, clarity, and smooth implementation.

This module begins by introducing the purpose and importance of architectural documentation. It emphasizes how clear documentation captures the system's structure, design decisions, and rationale, enabling teams to understand, maintain, and evolve the architecture over time.

Key documentation methods are explored, such as using **Unified Modeling Language (UML)** for creating visual representations of components, relationships, and workflows. The module also introduces the **C4 Model** (Context, Container, Component, and Code), a modern, lightweight approach to visualizing software architecture at different levels of detail.

Next, the module addresses communication strategies for architects. It covers techniques to present architectural decisions to technical and non-technical audiences, focusing on tailoring the message to their needs. Tools like architecture decision records (ADRs) are introduced to document trade-offs and reasoning behind key choices.

Finally, real-world case studies and examples demonstrate how clear documentation and communication prevent misunderstandings, reduce technical debt, and streamline development.

By the end of this module, learners will understand how to create concise, actionable documentation and communicate effectively with diverse audiences. These skills are essential for ensuring a shared understanding of the architecture, maintaining project alignment, and supporting long-term system success.

Lesson 8.1: Using UML for Architecture Modeling

Unified Modeling Language (UML) is a standardized visual language used to model the architecture and design of software systems. It provides a clear way to represent system components, their relationships, and workflows, making it easier for teams to understand and communicate architectural decisions.

Why Use UML for Architecture?

UML helps architects visualize and communicate complex systems by breaking them into manageable diagrams. This simplifies collaboration across teams and ensures everyone shares a common understanding of the system.

Key UML Diagrams for Architecture Modeling

1. **Component Diagram:**

   - Represents the high-level structure of a system by showing components, interfaces, and their dependencies.

   - **Use Case:** Illustrates how micro-services interact in a distributed system.

2. **Class Diagram:**

   - Shows the static structure of classes, their attributes, methods, and relationships.

   - **Use Case:** Modeling the core entities in a domain-driven design approach.

3. **Sequence Diagram:**

- Depicts the interaction between components or objects over time, highlighting the sequence of messages.

- **Use Case:** Modeling API calls between a client and server.

4. **Deployment Diagram:**

- Represents the physical deployment of software components on hardware nodes.

- **Use Case:** Visualizing cloud-based infrastructure or on-premises server configurations.

5. **Activity Diagram:**

- Shows workflows and processes within the system.

- **Use Case:** Visualizing the steps of a user registration process.

Best Practices for UML

1. **Focus on simplicity**; only include relevant details to avoid clutter.

2. Use **consistent notation** and legends to ensure clarity.

3. **Tailor diagrams** to your audience—detailed for developers, abstract for stakeholders.

Key Takeaways

UML provides architects with a powerful way to model systems visually, ensuring better communication and alignment across teams. By mastering key diagrams like component, class, and sequence diagrams, architects can clearly document and share their vision, leading to smoother project execution.

Lesson 8.2: The C4 Model: A Practical Approach

The **C4 (Context, Container, Component, Code) Model** is a modern, lightweight approach to visualizing and documenting software architecture. Developed by Simon Brown, it provides a hierarchical set of diagrams that represent a system at multiple levels of detail. This practical framework ensures that all stakeholders, from developers to non-technical executives, can understand the system's architecture.

The Four Levels of the C4 Model

1. **Context Diagram:**

   - **Purpose**: Provides a high-level view of the system and its interactions with users and external systems.

   - **Use Case**: Explains the system's scope and its role in the broader environment.

   Example: An online bookstore interacting with customers, a payment gateway, and an inventory system.

2. **Container Diagram:**

   - **Purpose**: Breaks the system into containers, such as applications, services, and databases, showing their responsibilities and interactions.

   - **Use Case**: Shows how key components communicate and where they are deployed.

Example: A web app interacting with a REST API and a database.

3. **Component Diagram:**

    - **Purpose**: Zooms into a specific container to show its internal structure and interactions between components.

    - **Use Case**: Helps developers understand how a container's logic is organized.

    Example: A micro-service's modules and their roles (e.g., order processing, logging).

4. **Code Diagram:**

    - **Purpose**: Offers the most detailed view, showing the implementation of a specific component.

    - **Use Case**: Provides guidance for developers during coding.

    Example: Classes and methods for processing payments.

Why Use the C4 Model?

- **Clarity Across Stakeholders**: Each level targets a different audience, from business leaders to developers.

- **Focus on Essentials**: Avoids overwhelming complexity by focusing only on key elements.

- **Scalability**: Works for small systems and large, distributed architectures alike.

Key Takeaways

The C4 Model bridges communication gaps in software architecture by presenting the system at varying levels of detail. Its practical, hierarchical approach makes it an invaluable tool for architects to document and explain architectures clearly and effectively.

Lesson 8.3: Best Practices for Communicating Architectural Decisions

Effective communication of architectural decisions is critical for aligning teams, managing stakeholder expectations, and ensuring successful implementation of a system's architecture. The following best practices help architects convey decisions clearly and ensure they are understood and supported.

1. Use Visual Models

Diagrams simplify complex ideas, making them easier to understand. Use tools like **UML**, the **C4 Model**, or flowcharts to illustrate components, workflows, and interactions.

- **Best Practice:** Tailor visuals to your audience; high-level diagrams for stakeholders and detailed ones for developers.

2. Document Decisions with Context

Use **Architecture Decision Records (ADRs)** to formally document key decisions. An ADR includes:

- **The Problem:** What challenge the decision addresses.

- **The Solution:** The chosen approach and its rationale.

- **Alternatives Considered:** Other options and why they were rejected.

- **Implications:** Potential trade-offs or risks.

This documentation ensures future teams understand the reasoning behind decisions, aiding maintenance and updates.

3. Tailor Communication to Your Audience

Different audiences require different levels of detail:

- **Non-Technical Stakeholders:** Focus on business impact, such as scalability or cost.

- **Developers:** Dive into technical details, such as APIs, patterns, or frameworks.

4. Encourage Feedback

Involve team members early in the decision-making process. Collaboration fosters buy-in and often leads to better solutions by incorporating diverse perspectives.

5. Be Transparent About Trade-offs

Architectural decisions often involve trade-offs. Clearly explain the compromises, such as prioritizing performance over maintainability or cost over scalability, to set expectations.

6. Keep Communication Iterative

Regularly revisit decisions as requirements and technology evolve. Share updates to maintain alignment across teams.

Key Takeaways

Clear, audience-specific communication and proper documentation of architectural decisions ensure alignment and transparency. By using tools like ADRs and visual models, fostering collaboration, and iterating decisions, architects can build trust and ensure the long-term success of their designs.

■■

ARCHITECTURE AND MODERN DEVELOPMENT PRACTICES

Explores how modern development practices influence software architecture, emphasizing the integration of agile methodologies, DevOps, and emerging tools. These practices reshape how architects design, build, and maintain systems, ensuring they remain flexible, scalable, and responsive to change.

This module begins by examining how **Agile methodologies** impact architecture. Agile prioritizes iterative and incremental development, requiring adaptive architectures that evolve over time. Concepts like evolutionary architecture and minimum viable products (MVPs) are discussed to highlight how architects can align with Agile goals.

Next, the module delves into **DevOps** and its effect on architectural decisions. Continuous Integration/Continuous Delivery (CI/CD) pipelines, containerization, and Infrastructure as Code (IaC) are explored as key practices. These tools demand architectures that support rapid deployment, automation, and seamless integration.

The module also highlights the role of **cloud-native architectures** in modern development. Concepts like micro-services, server-less computing, and Kubernetes-based orchestration are introduced, showing how they support scalability, resilience, and cost efficiency in today's dynamic environments.

Finally, the module discusses how testing strategies (e.g., automated testing and TDD) and monitoring tools integrate with architecture to improve system reliability and performance.

By the end of this module, learners will understand how modern development practices influence architectural design and implementation. They will be equipped to create systems that are agile-friendly, cloud-ready, and DevOps-compliant, meeting the demands of fast-paced, high-performance development environments.

Lesson 9.1: Integrating DevOps Principles into Architecture

DevOps is a modern approach that combines **development (Dev)** and **operations (Ops)** to enable faster, more reliable software delivery. Integrating DevOps principles into software architecture ensures that systems are scalable, maintainable, and deployable in automated, high-performance environments.

Key DevOps Principles

1. **Continuous Integration (CI):**
   Developers frequently integrate code changes into a shared repository, ensuring early detection of bugs.

2. **Continuous Delivery (CD):**
   Automates the process of deploying applications, making it easy to release updates anytime.

3. **Automation:**
   Automating repetitive tasks, such as testing, infrastructure provisioning, and monitoring, reduces errors and improves efficiency.

4. **Collaboration:**
   Bridging the gap between development and operations teams fosters better communication and faster problem resolution.

Architectural Considerations for DevOps

1. **Modular and Scalable Design:**

   - Use micro-services or modular architectures to support independent deployment and scaling.

   Example: In an e-commerce platform, deploying an updated product catalog service independently of the payment system.

2. **Infrastructure as Code (IaC):**

   - Design systems that support declarative infrastructure definitions (e.g., Terraform, AWS CloudFormation).

   - Ensures consistent environments across development, testing, and production.

3. **Automated Testing and Deployment:**

   - Architect applications to integrate with CI/CD pipelines.

   - Use tools like Jenkins or GitHub Actions for seamless build and deployment workflows.

4. **Observability and Monitoring:**

   - Build-in logging, metrics, and tracing to identify and resolve issues quickly.

   - Tools like Prometheus and ELK Stack can provide real-time insights.

Benefits of DevOps-Integrated Architecture

- **Faster Time to Market:** Enables frequent and reliable releases.

- **Improved Reliability:** Automation reduces human errors.

- **Scalability:** Modular systems scale seamlessly with demand.

- **Collaboration:** Teams work more effectively toward shared goals.

Key Takeaways

Integrating DevOps principles into architecture promotes agility, reliability, and scalability. By incorporating modular design, automation, and observability, architects can create systems optimized for rapid development and deployment in today's fast-paced environments.

Lesson 9.2: Infrastructure as Code (IaC): Concepts and Tools

Infrastructure as Code (IaC) is a practice that manages and provisions computing infrastructure through machine-readable scripts rather than manual configuration. By treating infrastructure like software, IaC enables consistency, automation, and scalability in modern development environments.

Key Concepts of IaC

1. **Declarative vs. Imperative Approach:**

   - **Declarative:** Specifies the desired state of the infrastructure (e.g., "Deploy 3 web servers").

   - **Imperative:** Defines step-by-step instructions to achieve the desired state (e.g., "Start a server, then configure it").

2. **Version Control:**
   IaC scripts are stored in repositories like Git, allowing tracking, rollback, and collaboration, just like code.

3. **Idempotence:**
   Applying the same script multiple times produces the same results, ensuring consistency across environments.

4. **Automation and Reusability:**
   IaC automates repetitive tasks (e.g., server provisioning)

and creates reusable templates for consistent deployments.

Popular IaC Tools

1. **Terraform:**

   - A declarative tool for managing infrastructure across cloud providers.

   Example: Deploying multi-cloud environments with a single configuration file.

2. **AWS CloudFormation:**

   - A native AWS tool for managing resources using JSON/YAML templates.

   Example: Automating setup for an AWS-based web application.

3. **Ansible:**

   - Focuses on configuration management and orchestration using YAML playbooks.

   Example: Setting up a load balancer and configuring servers simultaneously.

4. **Kubernetes and Helm:**

   - Kubernetes handles container orchestration, and Helm automates deploying configurations.

   Example: Scaling micro-services across clusters.

Benefits of IaC

- **Consistency:** Eliminates human error by automating infrastructure setup.

- **Scalability:** Easily replicate environments for scaling or disaster recovery.

- **Efficiency:** Speeds up deployments with reusable templates.

- **Collaboration:** Developers and operations teams share the same codebase for infrastructure.

Key Takeaways

IaC simplifies infrastructure management by automating provisioning and ensuring consistency across environments. Using tools like Terraform, Ansible, and CloudFormation, architects can design scalable, reliable systems while integrating seamlessly into DevOps workflows.

Lesson 9.3: Testing Strategies for Robust Architectures

Testing is essential to ensure that software architectures are **robust**, **reliable**, and meet both functional and non-functional requirements. Robust architectures require a **multi-layered testing strategy** that covers every aspect of the system, from individual components to the entire application.

Key Testing Strategies

1. **Unit Testing:**

   - Focuses on individual components or modules in isolation.

   Objective: Ensure that each unit of the architecture performs as expected.

   Example: Testing a data validation function in the business logic layer.

2. **Integration Testing:**

   - Verifies interactions between components and layers.

   Objective: Ensure proper communication between modules (e.g., APIs, databases).

   Example: Testing the interaction between a REST API and its database.

3. **End-to-End Testing:**

- Simulates real-world user workflows across the entire system.

Objective: Ensure the system works as intended from start to finish.

Example: Testing the entire checkout process in an e-commerce app.

4. **Performance Testing:**

   - Evaluates the system's speed, responsiveness, and stability under load.

   Example: Using tools like JMeter to test response times under heavy traffic.

5. **Security Testing:**

   - Identifies vulnerabilities in the system.

   Example: Running penetration tests to ensure data is protected against unauthorized access.

6. **Chaos Testing:**

   - Introduced in distributed systems to test resilience under unexpected failures.

   Example: Simulating server crashes in a micro-services architecture.

Best Practices for Testing Architectures

1. **Automate Wherever Possible:**
   Use CI/CD pipelines to automate testing, ensuring rapid feedback on code changes.

2. **Test Early and Often:**
   Shift testing left in the development process to catch issues early.

3. **Use Mocking and Stubs:**
   Simulate external dependencies during testing to isolate specific components.

4. **Monitor in Production:**
   Combine testing with real-time monitoring tools like Prometheus or Splunk to identify runtime issues.

Key Takeaways

A robust testing strategy involves multiple layers, from unit tests to chaos testing, ensuring every part of the architecture is reliable and resilient. By adopting automated tools and best practices, architects can design systems that handle real-world challenges with confidence.

■■

DOMAIN-DRIVEN DESIGN

Introduces **Domain-Driven Design (DDD)**, a software design approach that focuses on aligning technical systems with business domains. DDD emphasizes collaboration between developers and domain experts to create models that accurately represent business processes, ensuring systems meet real-world needs.

This module begins by explaining the core concept of domains—the areas of knowledge or activity relevant to a specific business. It introduces the idea of a ubiquitous language, a shared vocabulary used by both developers and stakeholders to avoid misunderstandings and bridge the gap between technical and business teams.

Next, the module delves into DDD's key building blocks:

- **Entities and Value Objects:** Fundamental objects in the domain model, representing data and behavior.

- **Aggregates:** Groups of related entities with clear boundaries, ensuring consistency.

- **Bounded Contexts:** Sections of the domain model defined by specific responsibilities, enabling scalability and modularity.

The module also discusses strategic design, which involves identifying and separating core domains (key business areas) from generic domains (supporting processes). This helps prioritize resources and focus efforts on delivering maximum business value.

By the end of this module, learners will understand how to use DDD principles to design systems that are scalable, maintainable, and aligned with business goals. Through real-world examples and exercises, learners will gain the skills to model complex systems effectively, communicate with stakeholders clearly, and build software that solves real business problems.

Lesson 10.1: Understanding Strategic Design and Bounded Contexts

Strategic Design is a key principle of **Domain-Driven Design (DDD)** that focuses on organizing and managing the complexity of large systems by aligning software design with business goals. Central to this concept is the idea of **bounded contexts**, which define clear boundaries within a system to ensure clarity and maintainability.

What is Strategic Design?

Strategic design emphasizes understanding the business domain and dividing it into **core**, **supporting**, and **generic** subdomains:

- **Core Domains:** The most critical business areas that differentiate the organization.

- **Supporting Domains:** Secondary areas that assist the core domain.

- **Generic Domains:** Common functionalities that are not unique to the business, such as authentication.

By identifying these domains, architects can prioritize effort and resources on the core domains that deliver the most value.

What are Bounded Contexts?

A **bounded context** is a logical boundary that encapsulates a specific part of the domain model. Each bounded context has:

1. Its own **domain model** tailored to a specific business need.

2. A **ubiquitous language** shared between developers and stakeholders within that context.

3. Clear interfaces to communicate with other contexts.

Why Use Bounded Contexts?

1. **Decoupling:** Each context operates independently, reducing complexity and enabling scalability.

2. **Flexibility:** Teams can work on different contexts without conflicts.

3. **Clarity:** Prevents overlapping definitions of concepts across contexts (e.g., "Order" may mean different things in a billing system vs. inventory management).

Example: E-commerce System

- **Core Context:** Product catalog (business differentiator).

- **Supporting Context:** Inventory management.

- **Generic Context:** Payment processing.

Each of these are designed and managed independently but integrates seamlessly with the whole system.

Key Takeaways

Strategic design and bounded contexts ensure that systems are modular, scalable, and aligned with business goals. By breaking down the domain into manageable parts, architects can focus on delivering value while minimizing complexity.

Lesson 10.2: Core Building Blocks: Entities, Value Objects, Aggregates

In **Domain-Driven Design (DDD)**, **entities**, **value objects**, and **aggregates** are the fundamental building blocks of a domain model. They help architects represent business concepts and maintain system integrity.

1. Entities

Entities are objects with a unique identifier that persists over time, regardless of changes to their attributes.

Characteristics:

- Have a unique identity (e.g., a user ID, product ID).

- **Mutable:** Their attributes may change, but their identity remains constant.

  Example:
  A "Customer" entity in an e-commerce system has a unique ID, but their name, address, or purchase history can change.

2. Value Objects

Value objects represent immutable concepts without unique identifiers. They are defined by their attributes rather than identity.

Characteristics:

- **Immutable:** Cannot be modified after creation.

- Lightweight and reusable.

   Example:
   An "Address" value object with properties like street, city, and zip code. Two identical addresses are considered equal, making them ideal for comparisons or calculations.

3. Aggregates

Aggregates are collections of entities and value objects bound together by a root entity (the **aggregate root**). Aggregates ensure consistency and integrity within their boundaries.

Characteristics:

- Changes to entities within the aggregate go through the aggregate root.

- Aggregates define transactional boundaries (e.g., a single database transaction).

   Example:
   An "Order" aggregate includes an order entity (aggregate root) and value objects like "OrderLine" and "Address." Any updates to the order must be handled through the aggregate root.

Why These Building Blocks Matter

1. **Entities** ensure identity and persistence over time.

2. **Value objects** provide immutability and simplicity.

3. **Aggregates** ensure consistency by defining clear boundaries.

Key Takeaways

Using entities, value objects, and aggregates helps architects **create robust, maintainable models**. Together, they clarify domain concepts, enforce consistency, and reflect real-world business rules, ensuring the system aligns with the domain's needs.

Lesson 10.3: Applying DDD to Solve Complex System Challenges

Domain-Driven Design (DDD) offers a powerful framework for addressing challenges in complex systems by aligning software architecture with business needs. Applying DDD principles helps architects **tackle complexity, improve collaboration**, and **create scalable, maintainable** systems.

Key Challenges in Complex Systems

1. **Ambiguity in Requirements:**
   Complex systems often involve diverse stakeholders, leading to unclear or conflicting requirements.

2. **Tightly Coupled Components:**
   Interdependencies between components make systems difficult to change or scale.

3. **Scaling Domain Knowledge:**
   Ensuring developers understand the business domain becomes harder as teams grow.

How DDD Addresses These Challenges

1. **Ubiquitous Language:**
   DDD emphasizes collaboration between developers and domain experts to create a shared language. This minimizes misunderstandings and ensures the domain model reflects real-world business processes.

   Example: Defining terms like "Order" or "Customer" consistently across teams.

2. **Bounded Contexts:**
By dividing the system into bounded contexts, DDD isolates different parts of the domain to reduce complexity. Each context is self-contained and interacts with others through well-defined interfaces.

> **Example:** In an e-commerce platform, separating "Inventory" from "Order Management" ensures scalability and clarity.

3. **Focus on Core Domains:**
DDD encourages prioritizing the most critical business areas (core domains) while delegating less important tasks (supporting or generic domains).

> **Example:** Optimizing the recommendation engine (core) while using off-the-shelf solutions for payment processing (generic).

4. **Aggregates for Consistency:**
Aggregates define clear boundaries for business rules and transactions, ensuring data integrity across the system.

> **Example:** An "Order" aggregate ensures all order lines and payments are consistent during updates.

Key Takeaways

By applying DDD principles like **ubiquitous language**, **bounded contexts**, and **aggregates**, architects can **simplify complex systems**, ensure scalability, and align the software with business objectives. DDD transforms challenges into opportunities by fostering collaboration and focusing on what truly matters.

■■

ABOUT THE AUTHOR

Amirul Sheikh is a distinguished Principal Software Engineer, Certified Software Architect, and a mentor with over 26 years of hands-on experience in the software industry. His expertise in modern C++ programming, object-oriented design, and software architecture has been honed through pivotal roles at Fortune 500 companies, including Oracle, GE, Verizon, and Hitachi Rail. Amirul's career showcases an impressive portfolio of accomplishments, from architecting scalable, high-availability distributed systems to leading cross-functional teams in delivering mission-critical software solutions.

As an author, Amirul has penned seminal works such as *Mastering Classic C++ Programming, Software Architecture: Create Software Like a Pro, Software Design Patterns: Design Software Systems Like a Pro, Algorithms Using C++*, and *Data Structures Using C++*. These books exemplify his deep technical knowledge and ability to simplify complex concepts for developers at all levels. His writing combines theoretical rigor with practical insights, making these resources indispensable for students, professionals, and anyone aiming to excel in software development.

In addition to his books, Amirul has created the video courses *Coding Confidence* and *High-Performance Programmer*, comprehensive learning programs distilled from his extensive industry experience. These courses guide learners through core software engineering principles, high-performance programming practices, and proven techniques for debugging and optimizing complex systems.

Amirul's passion for mentoring and education, coupled with his rich professional background, makes him a sought-after voice in the software development community. Through his books and courses, he empowers programmers to build robust, efficient, and future-proof software systems with confidence.

www.ingramcontent.com/pod-product-compliance
Lightning Source LLC
LaVergne TN
LVHW022347060326
832902LV00022B/4300